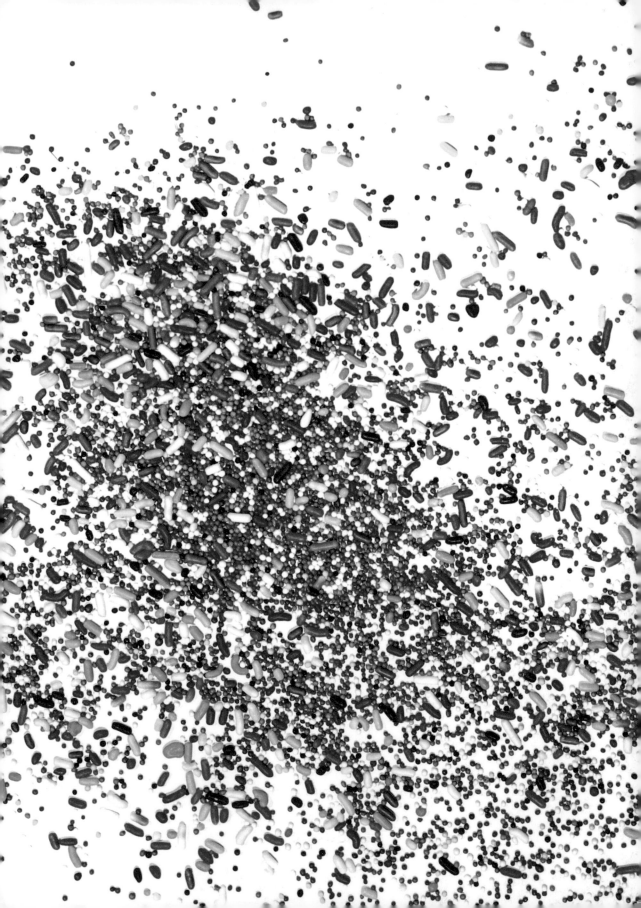

ALEX HOFFLER AND STACEY O'GORMAN

EVERYTHING SWEET

WITH PHOTOGRAPHS BY DAVID LOFTUS

SQUARE PEG

THIS BOOK AIMS TO
INSPIRE THOSE WHO
DARE TO DREAM. REACH
FOR THE RAINBOWS AND
YOU WILL FIND THAT
EVERYTHING IS SWEET.

CONTENTS

WOW, LOOK HOW FAR WE HAVE COME SINCE QUITTING OUR 9 TO 5 JOBS TO START UP THIS CRAZY MERINGUE ROLLER-COASTER JOURNEY!

We thought it was too good to be true when we got our first cookbook deal, and now here we are, two years later, with cookbook number TWO! Our first cookbook, *Meringue Girls Cookbook*, has now been published all over the world, from Italy and Germany, to America and New Zealand.

Finding a premises for our bakery was tough. We viewed so many different kitchens that weren't quite right, and we had almost lost all hope until we found the perfect space at 1 Broadway Market Mews. It had been recently used as a roti (deep-fried bread) factory, and was covered in so much grease and grime that you couldn't even see through the windows. With a lot of hard work and elbow grease, steam-cleaning, and a sprinkling of MG magic dust, we gutted and transformed the oily shell into our beautiful shiny workspace, where we now make all our lovely meringues, take masterclasses, do photo shoots, and run our office.

We have gone from being just us two gals, to having an entire team of incredible Meringue Girls. We now employ one head baker — the astonishing Sylvia Pearson — and have a team of eight other talented Meringue Girls helping to run the show. It's becoming a well-oiled meringue machine.

We are running regular masterclasses from our new bakery, which were rated by the *Evening Standard* as one of the best London-based foodie masterclasses. Our passion for street food and foodie events is also very much alive. We have a weekly market stall at Broadway Market, which we love. Plus we are now supplying heaps of great retailers, including Selfridges, Fortnum & Mason, Jamie Oliver's Recipease and Harvey Nichols, as well as being in recent talks about some super-exciting global franchising plans.

Our orders go up and up every week, and we are continuing to create bespoke sweet creations for high-end fashion brands & PR and press events.   >

Weddings are also a huge part of our work. We have teamed up with the lovely Carla at Fondant Fox to create amazing bespoke wedding and celebration cakes.

We are developing our passion for food styling and are now represented by the amazing HERS agency who've teamed us up with clients such as the BBC, *Wallpaper*, the *Guardian*, *Grazia*, Tesco, Morrisons and Green & Blacks.

Some recent highlights have been working with Selfridges to create an iconic Oxford Street shop window display of mountainous meringues, creating a Rainbow Bellini bar for Ab Fab Quaglino's, and making an appearance on Paul Hollywood's *Pies and Puds*, *Sunday Brunch* and *Alan Titchmarsh*. We were even lucky enough to be commissioned by Waitrose TV to present three short Christmas baking videos in our very own bakery. BASICALLY. SO. MUCH. FUN.

Stacey got married to the love of her life, Brady, and Alex got engaged to the man of her dreams, Neil — and had a beautiful baby Meringue Girl called Indi. We told you we have been busy!

From being completely clueless, carefree, and going into it all with a blind eye (seriously, what's a profit and loss sheet?!), we've worked hard, and have gained so much business knowledge along the way. Celebrating our wins, learning from our mistakes, and having a lot of fun doing it.

Our dedication in the first book was to everyone who dreams of leaving their 9 to 5. What makes us really happy is the feeling that we have inspired lots of people to bake, and even to take the plunge and start up their own baking business. We are so happy to read emails from people who are giving it a go. Our mantra will always be to inspire people to reach for their rainbow.

We seriously couldn't have done all this without the support of so many — who know who they are. From just 300 Instagram followers in 2013, to over 60,000 — thank you to all our supporters, we are so humbled every day. We want to say a huge thank you to David Loftus, who we truly believe set the wheels of this whole adventure in motion, by taking amazing photographs for our website, and Instagramming a few snaps — isn't social media a dream!

We absolutely love Instagram (to the point of addiction). It is a real hobby of ours to watch baking trends develop and new ideas flourish. We have been inspired by so many amazing people all over the world, and have attempted to credit the sources of our inspiration throughout the book. Go and check out their accounts, you won't be disappointed.

There is no stopping our momentum, and we have now set our sights high on Meringue Girls world domination. Who knows what wondrous things these next few years will bring, but one thing we do know is that we will be reaching for the rainbows.

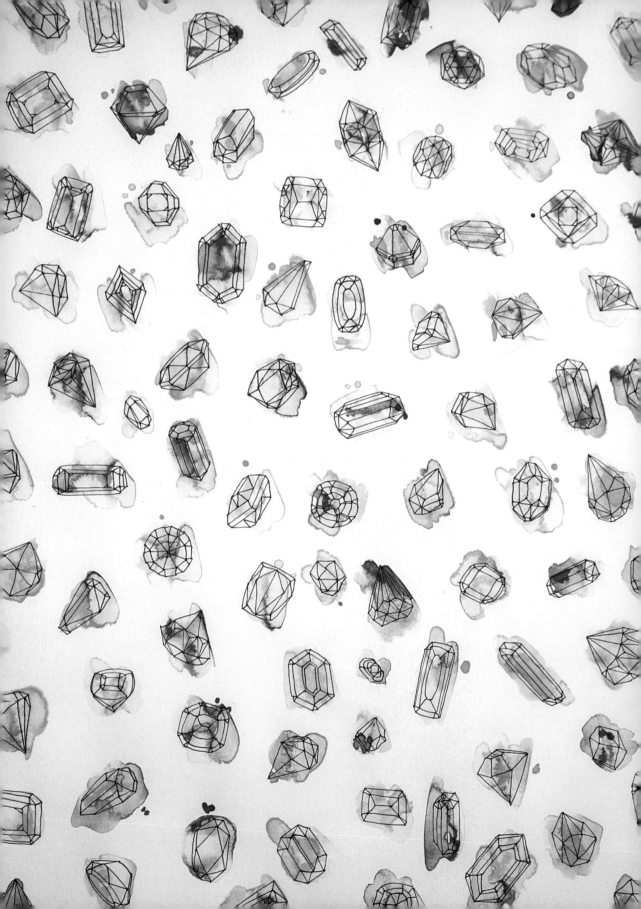

FANCY FLUMPS

MAKES 1 LONG ROPE

For the marshmallow dusting,
to stop everything sticking:
· 100g icing sugar
· 50g cornflour

For the marshmallow mixture:
· 70g free-range egg whites
  (approx. 2 large eggs)
· a pinch of table salt
· 350g caster sugar
· 12 leaves of gelatine
· 1 tbsp liquid glucose
· 150ml cold water

For the colouring:
· a few drops of pink food
  colouring (we use Sugarflair
  liquid colour in Hollyberry /
  Pink)
· a few drops of blue food
  colouring (we use Sugarflair
  liquid colour in Royal Blue)
· a few drops of yellow food
  colouring (we use Sugarflair
  liquid colour in Buttercup)

Equipment:
· a sugar thermometer
· disposable piping bags
· toothpicks

These marshmallow ropes are super fun to make. Marshmallows are made exactly the same way as an Italian meringue – adding hot sugar syrup to stiff egg whites – but with the addition of gelatine to make them set. We suggest making this with friends, as the marshmallow mixture sets quite quickly and you need a few hands on deck to pipe the ropes before it does. Good messy fun.

Prepare yourself:
Mix the icing sugar and cornflour together in a large bowl. Place a very long sheet of baking paper along your work surface. Using a sieve, dust very generously all over the baking paper with the icing sugar and cornflour mixture, reserving some of it for use later.

To make the marshmallow mixture:
Put the egg whites, salt and 1 tablespoon of the caster sugar into the bowl of a stand mixer, fitted with the whisk attachment, or use a clean glass bowl and a hand-held whisk. Don't start whisking yet.

Put the leaves of gelatine into a shallow bowl of cold water and leave them for 5 minutes to soak and become soft.

Meanwhile, put the liquid glucose and the 150ml of water into a heavy-based saucepan with the remaining caster sugar. Place over a medium heat and stir with a heatproof spatula to gently dissolve the sugar (this takes 5–10 minutes). Once the sugar has dissolved, turn up the heat and bring to the boil. Attach a sugar thermometer to the pan and continue to boil without stirring until the syrup reaches 120°C. Take the pan off the heat.

Now turn the mixer on to a medium speed and whisk the egg whites until stiff peaks form. Meanwhile, take the leaves of soaked gelatine out of the bowl and squeeze the excess water out, blotting them as dry as you can with a clean tea towel. Add to the hot sugar syrup and stir until the gelatine has completely dissolved.

Once the egg whites are at stiff peaks, crank up the whisk to a high speed while you add the hot syrup in a steady stream. Be careful to add the syrup directly to the egg whites, without it touching the side of the bowl or the whisk on the way down, otherwise it will cool before it hits the eggs.

CONTINUES OVERLEAF ›

_____

When all the sugar syrup has been added, continue to whisk on high speed for 5 minutes, until the mixture is cool and the bowl feels hand temperature. The mixture should be glossy and doubled in volume.

To colour:
This is a bit of a two-woman job. Very quickly, divide the mixture roughly between three bowls. To one bowl, add the pink colouring; to the next, add the blue; and to your final bowl, add the yellow. Stir quickly to evenly combine the colours, then transfer to three disposable piping bags.

Cut off a 1.5cm tip with scissors at the end of each bag (there is no need for a nozzle), and quickly get piping long straight ropes of marshmallow on to the dusted baking paper. Leave to set for 5 minutes, then lightly dust with a little more of your icing sugar and cornflour mixture. Leave the ropes to set until they are no longer sticky to the touch, and are easy to handle without breaking apart. This will take about 45 minutes to an hour. Don't leave them for too long, or they will set, becoming hard to twist, and may crack.

To twist those fancy flumps:
First, dust your hands with some of the remaining icing sugar and cornflour mixture. Now roll one rope of each colour back and forth in the mixture so that they are completely coated. Lay the three colours of rope side by side and skewer all three with a toothpick at one end. Carefully twist (or plait!) the ropes tightly, then skewer the other end with another toothpick to hold the twists in shape.

Repeat with all the ropes. They can be eaten immediately, but won't hold their twisty shape unless you let them set at room temperature for 24 hours to dry completely. The next day, remove the toothpicks and the twists will miraculously stay in their lovely shape.

The ropes will keep fresh for 1 week in an airtight container.

MARBLED MILLIONAIRE SLICE

For the base:
· 300g Lotus caramelised biscuits
· 120g unsalted butter, melted
· a pinch of sea salt

For the middle:
· 1 x 397g tin of sweetened condensed milk
· 80g soft brown sugar
· 3 tbsp golden syrup
· 100g unsalted butter

For the top:
· 200g dark chocolate (at least 70%), melted
· 100g white chocolate, melted
· pink oil-based food colouring (we used Wilton colours, but use them sparingly as they can affect the taste)

The most delicious combination of salty buttery Speculoos biscuit base, oozy caramel and beautifully marbled dark, white and PINK chocolate.

Preheat the oven to 180°C/gas 6. Grease a 20cm square baking tin and line with baking paper.

In a food processor, or using a rolling pin and a bag, crush the biscuits. Pour into a bowl with the melted butter, and fold through until well combined. Spoon into your baking tin and press down with the back of a metal spoon to flatten. Cover and refrigerate.

Over a low heat, combine the condensed milk, brown sugar, golden syrup and butter in a saucepan. Stir constantly with a wooden spoon until the mixture has thickened (about 5 minutes). Pour over your chilled base and distribute evenly. Chill completely before icing.

Smother the top of your slice with the melted dark chocolate. Randomly dollop half the melted white chocolate over the top of your dark chocolate layer. Colour the other half of your melted white chocolate with your pink oil-based colouring — you will need only a tiny amount of colour. Randomly dollop the pink over the white and dark chocolate, then, with a toothpick, swirl the colours together to produce your desired marbled effect.

Cover and chill in the fridge until the chocolate has completely set. Cut into slices with a hot knife.

JAMS

We've used our three favourite jam recipes throughout the book in a couple of different ways, but nothing beats hot freshly toasted sourdough smothered in butter with lashings of homemade jam. We live very close to an adorable jam shop – London Borough of Jam – run by Lillie, who hooked us up with these creations. She uses St John's doughnuts and fills them with her amazing jam concoctions – insane.

MAKES 675g

· 500g raspberries
· 400g jam sugar
· zest and juice of 1 lemon
· 100g soft liquorice
  cut into thin 0.5cm pieces

LIQUORICE AND RASPBERRY JAM

This jam has a sweet and zesty fresh raspberry flavour, with a subtle hint of aniseed. The pieces of liquorice don't dissolve completely which is a bonus, as we love getting a little surprise on our crumpet.

Place the raspberries and sugar in a large, heavy-based saucepan and bring to the boil. Now add the lemon zest, juice and liquorice.

Keep boiling gently until the jam has almost reached setting point — it should just coat the back of a spoon. It'll take about 20–25 minutes from when you add the liquorice. Make sure you don't reduce it too much, as you want your jam to be lovely and spreadable.

Place in sterilized jars and seal. To give as a gift, tie muslin around the lid of the jar with string, and tie on an old-school liquorice pipe.

MAKES 700g

· 625g ripe peaches
· 500g jam sugar
· 1 tbsp lemon juice
· 2 tbsp fresh thyme,
  finely chopped

PEACH AND THYME JAM

This jam is an amazing combination of savoury and sweet. We spoon it on to vanilla ice cream, spread it between layers of sponge cake and smother it on top of hot buttery sourdough.

De-stone and chop the fruit and place it in a large, heavy-based saucepan. Add the other ingredients, bring to the boil, then reduce the heat and simmer until soft and translucent.

Gently boil until the jam has almost reached setting point — it should just coat the back of a spoon. It'll take about 30–35 minutes. Make sure you don't

CONTINUES OVERLEAF ›

reduce it too much, as you want your jam to be lovely and spreadable, and it sets more as it cools.

Place in sterilized jars and seal. For a finishing touch, tie muslin around the lid of the jar with string, and attach a sprig of fresh thyme.

MAKES 600g

· **500g rhubarb**
· **500g jam sugar**
· **zest of 1 orange**
· **25g fresh ginger,**
  chopped finely
· **280g jar of stem ginger**
  (optional)

RHUBARB AND GINGER JAM

This rhubarb and ginger jam has beautiful tangy and spicy flavours, and is a classic combo. Pour the jam over balls of stem ginger for a gorgeous gift.

Slice the rhubarb into 2cm pieces. Place in a large bowl with the sugar, orange zest and fresh ginger. Stir the mixture so that everything is thoroughly combined, then cover and set aside for 40 minutes so that the sugar dissolves into the rhubarb juices, stirring after 20 minutes.

Tip the rhubarb mixture into a heavy-based saucepan and place on a medium heat. Stir and bring to the boil, then boil gently until the jam has almost reached setting point — it should just coat the back of a spoon. It'll take around 25 minutes. Make sure you don't reduce it too much — you want your jam to be lovely and spreadable.

Remove from the heat. Place a couple of balls of stem ginger into each sterilized jar, and fill with your jam. For a finishing touch, tie muslin around the lid of the jar with string, and attach a small stick of rhubarb if the gift is going to be given immediately.

NUT
BUTTERS

- 250g whole skin-on nuts (your pick of pistachios, whole almonds, hazelnuts, cashews, pecans)
- 1–2 tbsp vegetable oil or coconut oil
- a sweetener of your choice (agave syrup, honey, maple syrup or coconut sugar)
- sea salt, to taste

We're loving the influx of tasty new nut butters into the market, from pistachio, to almond, cashew and even homemade Nutella. Considering how easy they are to make, they are quite expensive to buy – so we decided to develop our own easy recipes. You can store them in your fridge for up to a month, spread them on toast, or add them to peanut butter cups – and they also make fantastic gifts.

First toast the nuts in a heavy-based frying pan until golden. This allows the flavour to develop and the oils to be released, which helps with the grinding.

Put the warm toasted nuts into a food processor and add 1 tablespoon of your chosen oil. Grind the nuts to a fine powder, leaving the mixer to run for 15—20 minutes, pausing regularly to scrape the sides of the bowl, until all the nuts have broken down into a creamy smooth paste. Add a little more oil if necessary, and continue to mix — have faith: it will come together.

Flavour to taste with your choice of sweetener (we like agave syrup) and season with sea salt. Pack into sterilized jars.

Try making your own Nutella — just make a batch of hazelnut butter and add 50g of melted milk chocolate and 25g of cocoa powder to the food processor at the end. It may seem a little runny at first, but let it chill in the fridge overnight, and it will become the perfect consistency.

JAMMIE DODGERS

MAKES 8

· 225g unsalted butter, at
  room temperature
· 125g icing sugar, plus
  extra for dusting
· ½ tsp vanilla bean paste
  (to make your own, see
  page 52)
· 2 medium egg yolks
  (keep the whites for
  meringue!)
· 300g plain flour
· 120g jam of your choice
  (see page 29)

Equipment:
· a 10cm round cookie
  cutter (with frilled edge,
  if you have it)
· a 3cm heart, kiss or star
  shape (for the centre hole)

These are a British and a Kiwi classic (although they are called Shrewsburys in New Zealand). They are absolutely delicious and you can get as creative as you like with them. Traditionally they are made with strawberry jam; however, we have made them with our lovely unusual homemade jams. They are super cute and a great gift idea.

Using a stand mixer, or a bowl and a hand-held electric whisk, beat the butter and icing sugar together until softened and combined. Add the vanilla, egg yolks and flour and continue to whisk together to make a soft dough. Shape into a flat disc, wrap in clingfilm and chill for at least 1 hour until firm.

Preheat the oven to 170°C/gas 5. Line two large baking sheets.

On a lightly floured surface, roll out half the dough to the thickness of a £1 coin. Using a 10cm cutter, stamp out 8 circles as your bases and place on one baking sheet. Roll out the other half and repeat the process to stamp out 8 circles for your lids. Use a smaller cutter to cut out the centre of each biscuit, and then place on the second baking sheet.

As you have handled the dough a great deal, chill both baking sheets of circles in the fridge for 15 minutes, to allow the butter to firm up again — trust us, it's worth it, as you will bake a better-shaped biscuit.

Bake the biscuits for 10–12 minutes, until pale golden, then remove from the oven and leave to cool and firm up on the baking sheets.

Place a tablespoon of jam in the centre of each base biscuit and spread it out a little. Press on the top biscuits and dust with a little more icing sugar, to serve.

Wrap any leftover shortbread dough in clingfilm and freeze for up to a month. Use it to make our cute iced gems (see page 59).

ORANGE, PISTACHIO AND CARDAMOM MARSHMALLOWY MERINGUE TEACAKES

MAKES 20

For the chocolate orange biscuit bases:
· 50g butter, softened
· 50g caster sugar
· 1 small free-range egg, beaten
· ½ tsp vanilla bean paste (see page 52)
· zest of ½ an orange
· 75g plain flour, plus extra for dusting
· 15g cocoa powder

For the cardamom marshmallowy meringue filling:
· ½ tsp cream of tartar
· 280g caster sugar
· 120ml liquid egg white or 4 medium free-range egg whites
· ½ tsp ground cardamom

For the chocolate orange and pistachio topping:
· 100g dark chocolate (70%), broken into pieces
· a few drops of orange extract
· 1 tsp vegetable oil
· a handful of slivered pistachios, finely chopped
· dried rosebuds (optional)

Equipment:
· a 5cm round cookie cutter
· disposable piping bags

We grew up on Tunnocks teacakes – always hoping for that bright red and silver foil wrapper in our lunchbox. This is our slightly grown-up version, with a Meringue Girls spin – the perfect edible gift, or after-dinner treat: a crunchy chocolate orange biscuit base, topped with a marshmallowy meringue kiss spiced with cardamom, dipped in dark chocolate.

This is one of the easiest meringue methods there is – everything goes into one bowl, and it's whisked over the heat until it's stiff and ready. So easy. The best thing about these is that you don't need to faff around with gelatine or use a teacake mould.

To make the chocolate orange biscuit bases:
Beat the butter and sugar until combined, either by hand or in a mixer on a low speed. Beat in the egg, vanilla and orange zest, then gently stir in the flour and cocoa powder. Divide the mixture in half, shape each piece into a flat disc, wrap them both in clingfilm and chill for 2–3 hours, until the dough has firmed up.

Preheat the oven to 180°C/gas 6, and line a large baking sheet with non-stick baking paper. Dust a work surface with flour and roll out one of the balls of dough to 5mm thick. Cut out 10 rounds, using a 5cm cutter (re-roll and cut out any excess dough), and place them on the baking sheet. Repeat with the remaining dough to make a total of 20 biscuit bases, and bake for 10 minutes, until cooked through. Leave to cool completely on the baking sheet.

To make the cardamom meringue topping:
Place the cream of tartar, sugar and egg whites in a heatproof bowl and add 1 tablespoon of tap water. Place the bowl over a pan of simmering water, over a very gentle heat, and beat with an electric whisk for 15 minutes, until the mixture forms stiff, shiny peaks. Remove from the heat and carefully fold in the ground cardamom.

Spoon into a disposable piping bag and cut a hole the size of a 50p coin in the tip. Pipe the mixture on to the biscuit bases in a smooth teardrop 'kiss' shape. Place the biscuits on a tray and put into the fridge to firm up the meringue, while you make the chocolate and pistachio coating.

CONTINUES OVERLEAF ›

For the chocolate:
Place the chocolate, orange extract and oil in a small heatproof bowl and gently melt over a pan of simmering water until smooth and shiny. Leave to cool at room temperature for 5–10 minutes, until thickened slightly.

To assemble:
Finally, holding your teacakes by the biscuit base, carefully dunk the meringue into the melted chocolate. Sprinkle with slivered pistachios and poke in a rosebud if using. Transfer the finished teacakes back to the fridge for an hour or so, until the chocolate has formed a hard shell. Enjoy!

We have started experimenting with rainbow teacakes — dipping the mallow into coloured white chocolate. Food for thought!

MARBLED PAPER CHOCOLATE BARS

We've fallen in love with the Mast Brothers' chocolate and their beautiful packaging, and wanted to create our own personalized chocolate bars. We have marbled our own paper, which is deceptively simple, and produces a wicked psychedelic effect, man.

   We have created our own chocolate bars with crunchy bits of peppermint, and also gone a bit coco loco with splattered coloured white chocolate bars.

Equipment:
· **A4 thin white card**
· **marbling paints (see suppliers, page 221)**

TO MARBLE YOUR CHOCOLATE WRAPPERS

To marble paper, fill a deep baking tin with cold tap water. Drip small dots of marbling paint on to the water — they are oil-based, so they will float — then use a toothpick, or the back of a spoon, to move and marble the floating pattern. When you are happy, carefully place the A4 card flat on the water, then pick it up and turn over to reveal the beauty. Leave to dry completely in a warm dry place. This can take up to three days.

MAKES 3 BARS

· **2 tbsp demerara sugar**
· **1 tsp peppermint or orange oil-based extract**
· **300g dark chocolate (70%)**

Equipment:
· **3 chocolate bar moulds**

TO MAKE YOUR OWN CHOCOLATE BARS

Put the sugar and your chosen extract into a small bowl and leave to soak for 5 minutes.

Melt the chocolate gently, using your chosen tempering method (see page 216). Add the soaked sugar granules to the melted chocolate. Carefully fill your chocolate bar moulds and leave to set at room temperature.

Once completely set, tap the mould and flip to release the bars. If you have tempered your chocolate correctly, the bars will release easily and be as shiny as a mirror.

Now wrap them in your gorgeous marbled paper.

To make rainbow, splatter or ombré faded chocolate bars, follow the instructions for how to colour white chocolate on page 75 and get artistic filling your chocolate moulds.

BANGIN' BLISS BALLS

MAKES 25

For the balls:
· 250g squishy fresh dates, stones removed (buy the fresh ones that aren't super dried out)
· 50g whole roasted almonds, skin on
· 50g whole roasted hazelnuts, skin on
· 1 tbsp cocoa powder (use cacao if you want to keep them 'raw')
· 100g desiccated coconut
· a pinch of sea salt

For the chocolate coating:
· 100g 70% dark chocolate
· a handful of coconut shavings (optional)
· a handful of goji berries (optional)
· a handful of shelled pistachios, chopped (optional)
· a pinch of sea salt (optional)

We are addicted to these little balls of bliss, which taste like decadent brownie bites but are actually packed with nutritious and delicious things. The blitzed-up dates, nuts, coconut and cocoa form a gooey mouthful of goodness that tricks the mind into thinking it's a full-on sin. Dipping them in a little melted dark chocolate and setting them in the fridge creates a bittersweet shell that reveals the super squidgy centre within. Sprinkle with Maldon sea salt for a salty sweet sensation.

You can use any combination of nuts you have in your cupboard: hazelnuts, almonds, pistachios, walnuts, cashews and Brazil nuts all work amazingly well. You can even add a few goji berries for an extra healthy kick. These make a fab after-dinner treat, or even an 11 a.m. pick-me-up (the way we have them at the bakery). They keep in the fridge for a week (if you are lucky enough to have any left).

Place the dates, almonds and hazelnuts in a food processor and blend to a paste. You might need to add a few splashes of water to help this along. Don't worry if the mixture isn't completely smooth, as it's nice to have a bit of crunch. Add the cocoa powder, coconut and salt, and blend again. Mix until everything is well incorporated and the mixture is nice and sticky.

Line a tray with baking paper. Take about 1 tablespoon of mixture at a time and roll into a truffle-size ball between your palms. Damp hands will help you to roll them smoothly. Place the balls on the lined tray and refrigerate for about 20 minutes, to harden slightly.

Meanwhile, melt the chocolate in a glass bowl over a pan of simmering water, making sure the bowl does not touch the water. Once the chocolate is completely melted, set aside to cool slightly.

One by one, dip the balls in the melted chocolate and use a spoon to transfer them back to the tray. Sprinkle with any chosen toppings, and refrigerate until the chocolate hardens.

UNICORN POO MERINGUES

MAKES 40

· **1 batch of Meringue Girls Mixture (see page 204)**
· **food colouring – in all colours of the rainbow! (unnatural: Wilton gel or Sugarflair paste/ natural: Lakeland)**
· **your choice of magical flavour, perhaps strawnana? (strawberry and banana – to do this, use a couple of drops of strong natural essence from Foodie Flavours, see suppliers, page 220)**
· **edible glitter**

Equipment:
· **disposable piping bags**

Everyone knows that unicorns poo rainbows, right? Well, they do. These are both magical and delicious.

Make your Meringue Girls Mixture.

Preheat the oven to 100°C/gas ½ and line a large baking tray with baking paper.

While your meringue mixture is whisking in the mixer, turn a piping bag inside out and paint thick stripes of all the colours of the rainbow from the tip to halfway down the inside of the bag — so that all the inside of the bag is coloured, and the colours are in consecutive stripes of pink, red, orange, yellow, green, blue and purple. Turn back the other way, ready to be filled.

Fold through the flavour, if using. Fill up the coloured piping bag with your meringue and cut a hole the size of a 50p coin in the tip of the bag.

Holding the piping bag with two hands, using your lower hand to guide and your top hand to apply pressure, pipe out little kisses or droplets. You want to pipe with at least a 2cm 'drop' from your tray to your piping bag tip to get the perfect shape. The best way to do it is to squeeze your piping bag, let go with your top hand, then pull the bag up to get the perfect kiss shape.

Sprinkle with edible glitter and then cook the meringue kisses for 35—45 minutes. You'll know they're cooked when the outside feels dry and they lift off the baking sheet with their bases intact.

Serve them immediately on a bed of candy floss. Or package them in cellophane gift bags and tie with a rainbow ribbon. They will keep well in a biscuit tin for 1 week.

HOMEBREWED VANILLA BEAN PASTE

MAKES 180g

· 6 vanilla pods
· 1 tbsp of vodka
· 170g agave syrup

This is so much better than the shop-bought stuff, and it's incredibly quick and easy to make. It packs a serious vanilla punch. The lovely Bianca Virtue was our inspiration on this one. It's fab to have in your fridge, and can be used for all our recipes which call for vanilla paste. We made a big batch and gave these out as Christmas gifts to all our baking buddies. Buy your vanilla pods from Amazon to keep the cost low.

Place all the ingredients, including the whole vanilla pods to get the maximum flavour, in a food processor, and purée until smooth. Place a fine mesh sieve over a bowl and press on the vanilla bean 'pulp' with the back of a spoon so that you get as much through the sieve as possible — you want all the vanilla seeds but not the husky outside.

Pour the vanilla paste into sterilized airtight bottles. Keeps for 2 months in the fridge.

FRUIT ROLL-UPS

These are great for the whole family, a perfect substitute for lollies and other naughty snacks. We have to tell you upfront that while these are super easy to make, they require a decent amount of baking time. As long as you can monitor your oven, it will do all the work for you. We haven't passed our purées through a sieve, as we love the texture of the seeds, but feel free to if you'd like yours to look smoother.

Each of the mixtures here makes two standard sized baking trays of roll-ups which can be cut to whatever size or shape you fancy. Feel free to play around with all sorts of great flavour combinations once you've got the hang of these.

Preheat the oven to 110°C/gas 1. Line your baking trays with clingfilm (the clingfilm won't melt in the oven as the temperature is so low). Ensure the clingfilm is as smooth as possible and that there is a little bit of overhang on each side of the tray — the overhang will help you peel off the roll-up. (When using clingfilm, it tends to stick to your fingers as you attempt to smooth it into place in the tray, so here's a little trick: wrap a small cloth around your finger as you press the clingfilm down into the corners and edges of the tray.)

Purée your chosen fruit in a blender. Add the lemon and agave/honey and blend until your purée is silky smooth. Sieve to remove the seeds if desired. Place in a saucepan and cook over a low heat, stirring now and again, until reduced by half and of a loose jam consistency. Taste, and add a little more agave or honey if you think it needs it. Spoon the mixture on to the prepared clingfilmed baking trays and use a mini palette knife to spread it really thin and evenly. It doesn't need to go to the edges of the trays — it just needs to be super-thin, almost a sheer consistency.

Cook the purée for 3—4 hours — the length of time is completely dependent on the type of fruit you use. It's done when the fruit isn't sticky any more, but is all completely the same, dark colour and peels off the clingfilm easily. Use scissors to cut the roll-ups into strips, place them on pieces of non-stick baking parchment the same size — and roll up. Secure with ribbon or twine. These keep for up to 3 weeks in an airtight container.

APPLE AND APRICOT

· 240g Granny Smith apples, peeled, cored and chopped
· 240g fresh apricots, chopped
· 1 tbsp lemon juice
· 1–2 tbsp agave syrup or clear honey

KIWI AND MANGO

· 240g fresh mango, peeled and chopped
· 240g kiwi fruits, peeled and chopped
· 1 tbsp lemon juice
· 1–2 tbsp agave syrup or clear honey

PEAR AND BLACKBERRY

· 240g ripe pears, peeled and chopped
· 240g blackberries
· 1 tbsp lemon juice
· 1–2 tbsp agave syrup or clear honey

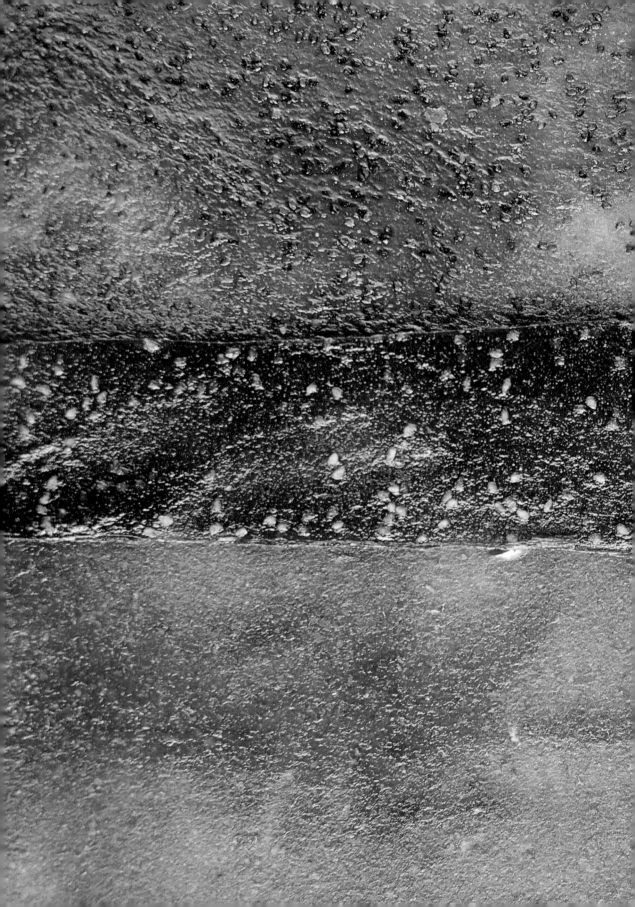

PAINT PALETTE ICED GEMS

MAKES 35

For the shortbread:
- 115g salted butter, at room temperature
- 35g caster sugar
- 50g cornflour
- 60g plain flour
- a pinch of salt

For the icing:
- 300g royal icing sugar
- a few tbsp tap water
- food colouring of your choice (unnatural: Wilton gel or Sugarflair paste/ natural: Lakeland. Use the Wilton gel sparingly as too much can affect the taste)

Equipment:
- a 3cm frilled cookie cutter
- disposable piping bags
- closed star piping nozzles (we used Wilton 2D nozzles)

These little iced gems are utterly nostalgic, and they are the perfect canvas for our colour obsession! In this recipe we have used a shortbread base, which we believe is so much tastier than your standard iced gem biscuit base. Of course we've gone all rainbow – you know us by now.

Preheat the oven to 150°C/gas 3 and line a flat baking tray with baking paper.

Cream the butter and sugar together until just combined, then sift in the cornflour and plain flour, add a pinch of salt and very gently fold, so that you have a very 'short' shortbread mixture. Chill the dough in the fridge for at least 30 minutes. Generously flour your work surface and roll out the chilled dough to 0.5cm thickness.

Use the cookie cutter to cut out little biscuits and gently place them on the baking tray, leaving a gap of at least 2cm between them, as they can spread. Gather up any scraps of dough, re-roll and stamp out as many biscuits as you can. Chill in the fridge for another 15 minutes until really cold while you clean up.

Bake the shortbread for about 15 minutes, until cooked but still pale in colour. To test, gently press down with your finger — the shortbread should give a little but still have some resistance. Leave to cool on the baking tray for a couple of minutes, before transferring carefully to a wire rack to cool completely.

Next, make the icing. Using a stand mixer, or a bowl and an electric hand-held mixer, sift the royal icing sugar and add a few drops of water at a time while beating slowly. If you add too much water the icing won't thicken as quickly, so take your time. Once incorporated, increase the speed of the mixer until the icing looks really white and forms stiff peaks.

If you are using more than one colour, divide your icing between the appropriate number of bowls. Add the different colours with the end of a toothpick, and mix until you get your desired shade. You will need to work quite quickly so that the icing doesn't form a hard shell. Prepare your piping bags and nozzles, and fill with icing. To finish your gems, hold the piping bag directly above the shortbread base and squeeze gently, then release the pressure before pulling the bag quickly up to create lovely little starred peaks.

The icing will harden further at room temperature. You can devour these nostalgic gems immediately, or bag them up when set and give them as lovely presents or wedding favours.

HONEYCOMBS

The honeycomb recipe is a miracle of science. Add a little baking soda to a sticky dark caramel and ta-daa! – you have yourself an incredibly crunchy, light and airy candy masterpiece. We have taken ours a step further by adding some winning flavour combinations. Perfect as a gift or to decorate cakes with.

MAKES A 20cm SQUARE SLAB

· butter, for greasing
· 100g hazelnuts, roasted and chopped
· 200g caster sugar
· 1 tbsp instant coffee
· 5 tbsp golden syrup
· 2 tsp bicarbonate of soda

Equipment:
· a square baking tin (approx. 20cm) – a silicone one is useful

---

HAZELNUT AND COFFEE HONEYCOMB

Line your tin with non-stick baking paper and grease the paper with butter. Scatter the chopped hazelnuts over the tray. (You can use a metal tin, but using silicone ensures the honeycomb stops cooking as soon as you pour it in.)

Mix the caster sugar, coffee and golden syrup in a deep saucepan (without allowing to bubble) over a medium heat. Once all of the sugar has dissolved, turn up the heat and simmer until the caramel resembles the colour of a copper penny. Take the pan off the heat and immediately add the bicarbonate of soda. Beat with a wooden spoon to fully incorporate it and the mixture is foaming. Scrape straight into the prepared tin - be careful as the mixture will be extremely hot.

Leave to harden at room temperature for about 1½ hours, then smash the honeycomb into pieces and enjoy.

MAKES A 20cm SQUARE SLAB

· butter, for greasing
· zest of 2 oranges, preferably in long strips
· 200g caster sugar
· 1 tsp ground cardamom
· 5 tbsp golden syrup
· 2 tsp bicarbonate of soda

Equipment:
· a square baking tin (approx. 20cm) – a silicone one is useful

---

ORANGE AND CARDAMOM HONEYCOMB

Line your tin with non-stick baking paper and grease the paper with butter. Scatter over the orange zest strips.

Mix the caster sugar, ground cardamom and golden syrup in a deep saucepan (without allowing to bubble) over a medium heat. Once all of the sugar has dissolved, turn up the heat and simmer until the caramel resembles the colour of a copper penny. Take the pan off the heat and immediately add the bicarbonate of soda. Beat with a wooden spoon to fully incorporate it and the mixture is foaming. Scrape straight into the prepared tin - be careful as the mixture will be extremely hot.

Leave to harden at room temperature for about 1½ hours, then smash up the hardened honeycomb into pieces and enjoy.

CONTINUES OVERLEAF ›

MAKES A 20cm SQUARE SLAB

· butter, for greasing
· 20g freeze-dried crispy
  rhubarb (from Souschef,
  see suppliers, page 220)
· 20g dried rose petals
  (from Souschef, see
  suppliers, page 220)
· 200g caster sugar
· 5 tbsp golden syrup
· 2 tsp bicarbonate of soda

Equipment:
· a square baking tin
  (approx. 20cm) – a silicone
  one is useful

RHUBARB AND ROSE HONEYCOMB

Line your tin with non-stick baking paper and grease the paper with butter.
Scatter over the rhubarb and rose petals.

Mix the caster sugar and golden syrup in a deep saucepan (without allowing
to bubble) over a medium heat. Once all of the sugar has dissolved, turn up
the heat and simmer until the caramel resembles the colour of a copper
penny. Take the pan off the heat and immediately add the bicarbonate of
soda. Beat with a wooden spoon to fully incorporate it and the mixture is
foaming. Scrape straight into the prepared tin - be careful as the mixture will
be extremely hot.

Leave the mixture to harden at room temperature for about 1½ hours, then
smash up the hardened honeycomb into pieces and serve rhubarb and
rose side up.

MAKES A 20cm SQUARE SLAB

· butter, for greasing
· 3 tsp dried or fresh
  lavender (see suppliers,
  page 220, or fresh from
  your garden)
· zest of 1 lemon
· 200g caster sugar
· 5 tbsp golden syrup
· 2 tsp bicarbonate of soda

Equipment:
· a square baking tin
  (approx. 20cm) – a silicone
  one is useful

LAVENDER AND LEMON HONEYCOMB

Line your tin with non-stick baking paper and grease the paper with butter.
Scatter over the lavender and lemon zest.

Mix the caster sugar and golden syrup in a deep saucepan (without allowing
to bubble) over a medium heat. Once all of the sugar has dissolved, turn up
the heat and simmer until the caramel resembles the colour of a copper
penny. Take the pan off the heat and immediately add the bicarbonate of
soda. Beat with a wooden spoon to fully incorporate it and the mixture is
foaming. Scrape straight into the prepared tin - be careful as the mixture will
be extremely hot.

Leave the mixture to harden at room temperature for about 1½ hours, then
smash into chunks.

TRICK
OR TREAT?

**MAKES 40
PER BATCH OF
MERINGUE GIRLS
MIXTURE**

For the pumpkins:
· orange food colouring
  (for a vivid orange use
  Sugarflair or Wilton gel
  paste. Use the Wilton
  gel sparingly or it may
  affect the taste)
· 50g dark chocolate
· 1 batch of Meringue Girls
  Mixture (see page 204)

For the ghosts:
· 50g of dark chocolate
· 1 batch of Meringue Girls
  Mixture (see page 204)

Equipment:
· disposable piping bags
· a small thick paintbrush
· toothpicks

We love Halloween! Well, any excuse to indulge our sweet tooth without feeling guilty. We also love any reason to get a bit creative with our Meringue Girls Mixture. These ghosts and pumpkins are uber cute. Boo!

To make the pumpkins:
Make a batch of Meringue Girls Mixture (see page 204).

Turn your oven to 100°C/gas ½. Line a large flat baking tray — use some of the meringue mixture to dollop on the four corners, and stick your baking paper securely in place.

Working quickly so that your meringue mixture does not deflate, turn a disposable piping bag inside out and use a paintbrush to completely cover the inside of the bag from tip to midway with orange food colouring.

Now turn the piping bag right side out and carefully spoon in your stiff meringue mixture. You need to pack the mixture in tightly — give it a good shake so there are no air bubbles. With sharp scissors, cut a hole the size of a 50p coin in the tip of the piping bag.

Hold the piping bag with two hands, using your lower hand to guide and your top hand to apply pressure, and pipe out little kisses. For the pumpkins, you want to make the bases a bit fatter than our standard kisses. You want to pipe with at least a 3cm gap from the tray to the tip of your piping bag to get the perfect shape. The best way to do this is to squeeze your piping bag from the top, let go with your top hand, then pull the bag up to get the perfect little kisses with peaks.

Bake in the oven for 35—45 minutes, or until the bases come off the baking paper intact.

Melt the dark chocolate in a heatproof bowl either in the microwave on a very low setting or over a saucepan of simmering water, stirring frequently. Dab the end of a toothpick into your melted chocolate and draw on spooky pumpkin faces. Leave to dry, then package them up.

CONTINUES OVERLEAF ›

To make the ghosts:
Make a batch of Meringue Girls Mixture (see page 204).

Turn your oven to 100°C/gas ½. Line a large flat baking tray — use some of the meringue mixture to dollop on the four corners, and stick your baking paper securely in place.

Spoon your stiff meringue mixture into the piping bag. You need to pack the mixture in tightly — give it a good shake so there are no air bubbles. With sharp scissors, cut a hole the size of a 50p coin in the tip of the piping bag.

Hold the piping bag with two hands, using your lower hand to guide and your top hand to apply pressure, and pipe out little kisses or droplets. You want to pipe with at least a 3cm gap from the tray to the tip of your piping bag to get the perfect shape. To give your ghosts a rippled belly effect, start piping a kiss as normal but don't lift the piping bag away. Instead, lift the bag only a tiny amount and then lower it back down again as you squeeze a second time. Repeat the lifting and lowering and then squeeze one final time. Stop squeezing and lift the bag to give your ghosts a lovely peak.

Bake in the oven for 35–45 minutes, or until the bases come off the baking paper intact, then set aside to cool.

While they cool, melt the chocolate in a heatproof bowl either in the microwave on a very low setting or over a saucepan of simmering water, stirring frequently. Draw on your scary ghost faces with the melted chocolate, using the handle of your paintbrush or a toothpick. Let them dry, then package them up.

Trick or treat? (Obvs treat!)

AFGHAN COOKIES

MAKES 16

For the biscuits:
· 170g butter, softened to
  room temperature
· 100g soft dark brown sugar
· 180g plain flour
· 3 tbsp cocoa powder
· ½ tsp baking powder
· a pinch of salt
· 60g Crunchy Nut Cornflakes,
  crumbled into small bits

For the icing:
· 45g caster sugar
· 45g butter
· 190g icing sugar
· 3 tbsp cocoa powder
· 12 walnut halves, lightly
  toasted for extra flavour
· a sheet of edible gold
  leaf (optional)

This is a rich, chocolatey, Crunchy Nut Cornflake cookie, drizzled with thick chocolate icing and topped with a walnut. The biscuit base is salty, crunchy and soft. It's a classic New Zealand treat, and they need to become a worldwide phenomenon – as they are delicious! They are also a great store-cupboard rainy day recipe, because you will already have most of the ingredients and you don't need real chocolate (which never lies around for long in our cupboards).

To make the biscuits:
Preheat the oven to 180°C/gas 6 and line two baking sheets with baking paper.

Cream the butter and brown sugar until just combined — do not over-mix. Sift in the flour, cocoa, baking powder and salt, and gently mix together. Then fold in the crushed cornflakes to form a thick crumbly dough. Roll into small golfball shapes using your hands and place on the baking sheets. Tap them down gently into discs about 6cm across. They don't spread very much in the oven.

Bake for 12–14 minutes, then leave to cool.

To make the icing:
Put the caster sugar and butter into a saucepan with 3 tablespoons of water and heat gently until the butter and sugar have melted to a syrupy consistency.

Sift the icing sugar and cocoa into a medium bowl. Pour the buttery sugary syrup on to the sifted icing sugar and cocoa and mix with a balloon whisk. Add 2–3 tablespoons of hot water to bring the icing together until you get a nicely shiny and drizzle-able consistency.

Drizzle the icing over the centre of each cookie and finish with a walnut half. If you feel like you need some gold leaf in your life — and let's face it, who doesn't? — use a dry paintbrush or mini palette knife to lift small pieces on to the walnut halves. If you have trouble getting the gold leaf to stick, dab a bit of water on to the walnut and it'll cling no probs. Leave to set, or munch immediately!

PISTACHIO, ORANGE AND COCONUT FLORENTINE STICKS

MAKES ABOUT 8 STICKS

· 100g butter
· 100g golden syrup
· 100g demerara sugar
· zest of 2 oranges
· 50g glacé cherries, chopped
· 100g coconut flakes
· 50g flaked almonds
· 50g pistachios, roughly chopped
· 100g plain flour
· 100g dark chocolate (at least 70%)

These are hands down the best Florentines we have ever tasted. The orange zest permeates the entire cookie and works so wonderfully with the rich dark chocolate, sour glacé cherries and nutty flavour. We've cut our Florentines into long sticks, which are ideal to serve with an espresso after a big meal.

Preheat the oven to 180°C/gas 6. Grease a large baking tray and line with non-stick baking paper.

Put the butter, golden syrup, sugar and orange zest into a small, heavy-based saucepan on a very low heat, and keep stirring until melted. Take off the heat and fold in the chopped glacé cherries, coconut flakes, flaked almonds, pistachios and flour.

Pour the mixture on to your lined baking tray and spread it out evenly. Bake for 8—10 minutes, or until golden. It will spread across the whole tray.

Take out of the oven and leave to sit in the baking tray for a few minutes before cutting into long strips. The tray must still be warm when cutting, otherwise the mixture becomes too brittle. Transfer your Florentines to a cooling rack.

To finish, melt the chocolate in a bowl over a saucepan of barely simmering water, making sure the base of the bowl doesn't touch the water — or melt gently in the microwave, stirring frequently. Place the cooled Florentine sticks base down on the wire rack and, using a teaspoon, splatter the tops with your melted dark chocolate.

Leave the chocolate to set completely.

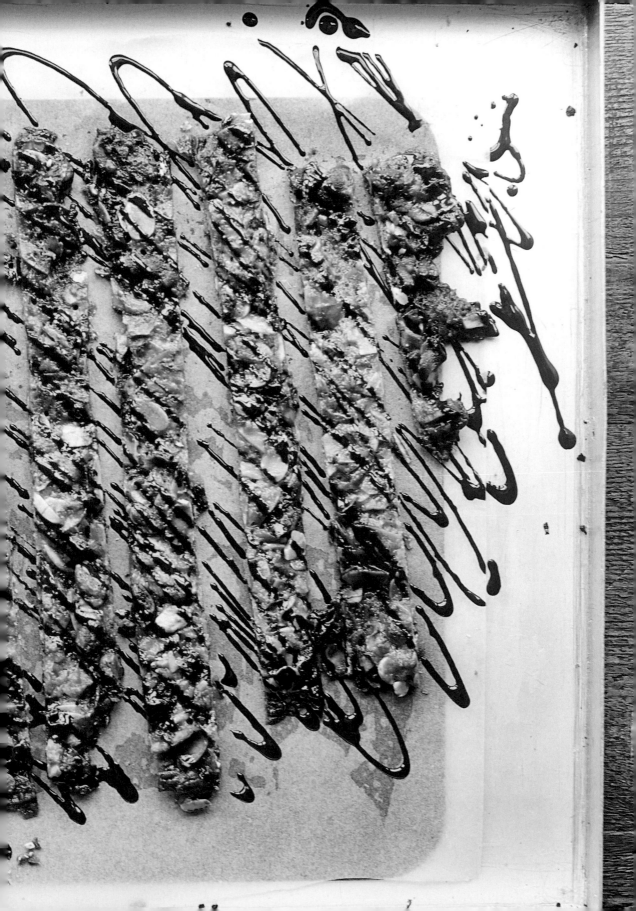

WHITE CHOCOLATE AND OREO PYRAMIDS

MAKES 15 PYRAMIDS

· 275g high-quality white
  chocolate, chopped
  into very small pieces,
  or use tempered white
  chocolate drops
· Wilton oil-based food
  colouring, used sparingly
  because it can affect
  the taste
· a handful of Oreo
  biscuits, whizzed whole
  to a fine powder, cream
  centre and all
· edible gold or silver leaf
  (optional)
· flavours (optional),
  e.g. oil-based extracts
  like watermelon, orange
  or peppermint
· freeze-dried fruits
  (optional), e.g. raspberry
  or strawberry pieces

Equipment:
· a 15-hole silicone pyramid
  chocolate mould (see
  suppliers, page 221 – you
  can use any type of
  chocolate mould, and
  silicone ice cube trays work
  really well; just make sure
  whatever mould you choose
  is very clean and dry)

We first discovered colouring white chocolate from a beautiful Instagram page – Nectar & Stone in Melbourne – and we have enjoyed experimenting with heaps of different mould shapes: discs, pyramids, chocolate bars, chocolate letters and 3D gem stones. Colouring chocolate is a real trend at the moment and we predict it will be the next craze.

Adding a colourful twist to white chocolate is super easy – from subtle ombrés, to a full-on rainbow. For this recipe you should use only oil-based food colouring. Water-based food colours have a habit of seizing within the mixture, making the chocolate grainy and unusable. We've used Wilton Primary oil colours to achieve the most vivid of shades.

Tempering your white chocolate is essential to get a really shiny finished product. If you don't temper, your chocolate will be soft and sticky when set. You can use our easy-peasy method (see page 217).

First you need to temper your white chocolate (see pages 216–217). Then, working very quickly, add a couple of colour drops to the melted chocolate and stir to achieve your desired colour. To fill the moulds with the layered Oreo effect, pour some chocolate into the base of the mould, crumble over a thin layer of finely crushed Oreos, then fill to the top of the mould with more melted chocolate. You can experiment with different coloured bases and tops, and with ombré fades within the chocolates (see page 112), by layering in the mould.

When you have finished, smooth off the top of each chocolate with a palette knife, and gently tap the silicone mould on the table to release any air bubbles. Leave to set in a cool place, not in the fridge, for at least 1 hour. (You should leave real tempered chocolate to set at room temperature, as it may lose the wonderful tempered shine you have created if you put it in the fridge.) Once set, pop the pyramids out of the moulds and keep in a cool place.

You can stir flavours into these chocolates too — just make sure you use oil-based extracts without alcohol, to ensure the chocolate doesn't seize. You can also add freeze-dried fruits if you like, such as raspberry and strawberry.

To finish, you can add a touch of edible gold or silver leaf on the top of each pyramid once they are set. Gold leaf is very fragile, so carefully dab the chocolate with a wet finger and apply a small piece of gold leaf with tweezers or a dry paintbrush. Package in chocolate boxes for a simply stunning gift.

EDIBLE FLOWER LOLLIPOPS WITH SEXY SHERBET

MAKES 18

For the edible flower lollipops:
· 225g granulated sugar
· 100ml glucose syrup
· 60ml water
· a couple of drops of natural passion fruit essence (or any other essence you desire! There are lots to choose from at Foodie Flavours, see suppliers, page 220)
· edible flowers

For the sherbet:
· 300g icing sugar
· 1 tbsp citric acid
· 1 tsp bicarbonate of soda
· 3 tbsp freeze-dried fruit pieces (e.g. raspberry or strawberry)

To dip:
· shop-bought or homemade lollipop sticks, or liquorice wands for a classic dib-dab experience (see suppliers, page 221)

Equipment:
· a pastry brush
· a sugar thermometer
· lollipop sticks
· silicone mat

These gorgeous homemade lollipops make perfect wedding favours; each one personalized with a name tag. We've made edible pansy lollies, but you can use any edible flowers you can get your hands on – such as violets or roses. They also taste delicious combined with our sexy sherbet! This is an incredibly quick and easy recipe that creates a mouth-twisting, fizzing, nostalgic sherbet that can be used with liquorice or lollipops. A fab gift for a kids' party bag, or for a sweet trip down memory lane.

The three key elements of sherbet work together to create a perfect balance: icing sugar for sweetness, citric acid for sourness and bicarbonate of soda for fizziness. You can add freeze-dried fruits for flavour and colour, adjusting the amounts of each to get your favourite flavoured old school treat.

Combine the sugar, glucose syrup and water in a saucepan over a medium heat and stir until the sugar dissolves. When it comes to the boil, dab a pastry brush into a cup of tap water and brush down the sides of the pan just above the boil line to remove any sugar crystals that have formed.

Attach a sugar thermometer to the pan and allow the mixture to continue to boil, without stirring, until it reaches 154°C. Immediately remove from the heat. Add a few drops of your chosen flavouring and stir to combine.

You need to work quickly to form your lollies. On a silicone mat or a sheet of baking paper, put a blob of sugar syrup down and use the back of a spoon to smooth it out into a circular shape. Add a lollipop stick, then put an edible flower on top. Finish by covering the flower completely with more sugar syrup.

Allow to cool for 30 minutes at room temperature. Wrap the lollipops individually in cellophane, tie with string and store at room temperature for up to a month. They are sticky, so keep them separate from each other.

To make the sherbet, simply whiz all the ingredients in a food processor or mix together in a bowl to form a fine dust.

To serve up a sherbet fountain, fill a small shot glass with sherbet, place a liquorice stick or lollipop in the middle, and get fizzy.

BANANA AND HAZELNUT DREAM CAKE WITH BROWN BUTTER ICING

SERVES 12

For the banana and
hazelnut cake:
· 500g (about 5 or 6) ripe
  bananas, peeled
· 125ml vegetable oil
· 125g soft light brown sugar
· 2 large free-range eggs
· 150g skin-on hazelnuts
· 200g self-raising flour
· 1 level tsp bicarbonate
  of soda
· 1 level tsp baking powder
· 1 level tsp ground cinnamon
· a pinch of sea salt

For the brown butter icing:
· 150g unsalted butter
· 500g icing sugar
· 4 tbsp whole milk

For the salted caramel sauce:
· 100g soft light brown sugar
· 50g golden syrup
· 75g unsalted butter
· 75ml double cream
· 1 tsp sea salt

For the banana caramel
shards:
· 200g caster sugar
· 50g banana chips

This is the best banana cake recipe of all time. The brown butter icing is a perfect combination with the gooey banana sponge.

We have decorated our cake with chocolate and hazelnut meringue bark, banana chip caramel shards, chocolate kisses, white chocolate Oreo pyramid bites, and salted caramel drips – inspired by the oh-so-cool Katherine Sabbath.

To make the cake:
Preheat the oven to 170°C/gas 5. Line the base of two 18cm round cake tins with baking paper, and grease the sides of the tins with butter.

Put the ripe bananas into a bowl and mash with a fork, keeping some bits chunky and some smooth. Using a stand mixer, or a large bowl and an electric whisk, beat the oil and the sugar, then add the eggs one at a time. Beat for 5 minutes, until you get a thick and creamy mixture.

Meanwhile roast the hazelnuts in a dry frying pan until they are nice and toasted. Then roughly chop, leaving some whole, some super-chunky and some fine. Add the mashed banana, nuts, sifted flour, bicarbonate of soda, baking powder, cinnamon and salt to the egg mixture and gently mix everything together until just combined, making a smooth batter.

Spoon the mixture into your prepared cake tins and bake for 40—50 minutes, or until a skewer or small knife comes out clean. It's all right if the middle is still slightly undercooked, as the cakes will continue to cook a little in the hot tins. Cool completely.

To make the brown butter icing:
Melt the butter in a small saucepan, then keep it cooking on a low temperature until it starts to turn a lovely nutty golden brown. Keep a close eye on it, as once it starts to turn colour, it turns quickly! You don't want to fully blacken the butter, just turn it a deep golden colour. Take it off the heat.

Using a stand mixer, or a large bowl and a wire whisk, sift the icing sugar and then begin to add a gentle stream of the hot melted butter. Slowly incorporate all the butter — the mixture will be very thick and lumpy. Now slowly add a few splashes of milk to loosen and smooth out the mixture, until you get a nicely fluffy consistency for icing your cake. The icing may seem to split at first, but just keep adding milk until it becomes perfectly smooth.

CONTINUES OVERLEAF ›

To decorate:
· white chocolate pyramids
  (see page 75)
· meringue shards
  (see page 191)
· chocolate meringue kisses
· (see page 207)
· shavings of dark chocolate
· extra banana chips

You can make the icing up to 3 days in advance, and store it in a clingfilmed bowl in the fridge.

To make the salted caramel sauce:
Melt the sugar and syrup with a few splashes of water in a small heavy-based pan and let it simmer for 3 minutes, stirring until you have a smooth caramel. Add the butter, cream and salt and stir (be careful, as the mixture will foam slightly and the sugar will be super-hot). Cook for another minute on the stove over a low heat, until thickened. Pour into a bowl and let it cool completely. You can keep any extra sauce to serve with a slice — it will keep in a sterilized jar in the fridge for 2 weeks.

To make the banana caramel shards:
Put the caster sugar into a heavy-based dry frying pan, and heat gently until it melts and turns a golden-brown colour. Quickly pour it on to a lined and greased baking tray, spread out thinly using the back of a spoon, and scatter with banana chips. Put into the fridge to set. Once cooled, break into large uneven shards. You can make these up to a week in advance, and keep them in a biscuit tin in a cool, dry place.

To assemble:
Once the cakes are cool, remove them from the tins and cut each one in half horizontally, so that you have four layers. Using half your brown butter icing, thickly ice one layer at a time, adding a swizzle of salted caramel to each layer and stacking them up tall. With the remaining icing, smother the whole cake, top and sides, then smooth off with a palette knife. Once you have completely iced your cake, drizzle the rest of the salted caramel sauce over the top, carefully pushing the sauce over the edges for that perfect drizzle look.

Decorations (optional!):
For a real wow-factor, we've gone to town with the decorations on this cake — add as much or as little decoration as you like, and by all means keep it low-key if you prefer. To assemble the cake as we've done, carefully stick your meringue and caramel shards right in the top of the cake — you may need to make a little incision so they go in neatly and stay upright. Then scatter meringue kisses, dark chocolate shavings, banana chips and white chocolate pyramids around the shards.

Your cake is now ready to be admired and devoured!

PISTACHIO CAKE WITH FRESH HONEYCOMB

SERVES 12

For the cake:
- 300g shelled pistachios
- 1 tsp gluten-free bicarbonate of soda
- a big pinch of sea salt
- 100g polenta
- 75g unsalted butter
- 150ml extra virgin olive oil
- 4 medium free-range eggs
- 200g golden caster sugar
- juice and zest of 1 lemon
- a drizzle of runny honey

For the pistachio buttercream:
- 150g unsalted butter
- 300g icing sugar
- 1–2 tbsp milk
- 3 tbsp pistachio nut butter (see page 33)

To decorate:
- extra pistachios and pistachio slivers (see suppliers, page 220)
- approx. 300g fresh honeycomb (in a jar of honey

Equipment:
- 23cm round springform cake tin

A dense and incredibly moist cake, with an intense roasted pistachio flavour. It is gluten free, and is perfect 'naked' with a dollop of Greek yoghurt and an afternoon cup of tea. Alternatively, combined with the homemade pistachio nut butter icing and fresh honeycomb, it makes for an amazing eating experience.

To make the cake:
Preheat the oven to 170°C/gas 5. Grease and line a 23cm round springform cake tin.

Spread the pistachios on a baking tray and toast in the oven for 5 minutes. Remove and cool slightly, then place in a food processor and grind to a fine powder. (You could also make the pistachio nut butter for the icing now, see page 33.)

Add the bicarbonate of soda, salt and polenta to the pistachio powder and mix to combine.

Put the butter and olive oil into a small pan on a low heat until the butter has just melted — don't allow it to boil.

Whisk the eggs and sugar together until pale and thick enough to slowly fall off the whisk in a ribbon. With the whisk still running, very slowly drizzle in the butter and oil mixture, whisking it into the eggs and sugar until fully incorporated. Add the lemon zest, and finally gently fold the nut and polenta mixture through until everything is just combined.

Pour into your prepared tin and bake for 45–50 minutes. Check that a skewer comes out clean and the surface springs back a little when you press it in the centre. The cake will be risen and golden, but it often cracks or sinks in the middle because it's gluten free — don't worry about this if it happens, it adds to its rustic delicious charm.

Mix the lemon juice and honey together, drizzle over the hot cake and let it soak in. Leave the cake to cool slightly in the tin, then remove and cool completely on a wire rack.

CONTINUES OVERLEAF ›

————————

This cake is delicious as it is, so feel free to serve it up naked with just a drizzle more honey, a dollop of yoghurt and some whole pistachio nuts. However, adding a pistachio buttercream just takes it one step closer to heaven!

To make the pistachio buttercream:
Whip the butter and icing sugar with an electric whisk until pale and fluffy, adding a touch of milk to loosen if necessary. Then fold in a few tablespoons of pistachio nut butter.

To serve:
Spread the pistachio buttercream over the top of the cake, then decorate with chunks of fresh honeycomb and whole and slivered pistachios.

FONDANT FOX CAKE

SERVES 12

For the cake:
- 2 x 410g tins of apricot halves in juice (480g total drained weight)
- 400g unsalted butter, softened and cut into small chunks
- 400g golden caster sugar
- 6 medium free-range eggs
- 150g ground almonds
- 1 tsp almond extract
- 300g self-raising flour
- 1 tsp table salt

For the filling:
- 600g double cream
- 3 tbsp icing sugar
- a few big tbsp nice-quality chunky apricot jam (or the peach and thyme jam on page 29)
- a handful of flaked almonds, toasted

This is a proper golden gem of a cake – a right old bobby-dazzler. It's a delicious apricot and almond sponge, filled with apricot jam, toasted almonds and cream, and covered with edible sequins for some serious glitz and glamour. This is the perfect birthday cake for those magpie friends who love a bit of bling. If you are not feeling as sparkly as that today, just top it with toasted flaked almonds for a delicious teatime cake.

In 2014 we began working really closely with Carla, from Fondant Fox, who really helped us on the shoot for the book, so we have dedicated this cake to her. (See how to make the edible origami foxes on page 192.)

To make the cake:
Preheat the oven to 160°C/gas 4. Line two round 18cm cake tins with baking paper.

Drain the tinned apricots in a sieve and cut into smaller chunks. Discard (or drink!) the juice. Dry them on kitchen paper, then dust them with a tablespoon or two of flour (this will help them not to sink during baking).

Using a stand mixer, or a large bowl and an electric whisk, beat the butter and sugar until light and fluffy. Beat in the eggs slowly, one at a time. Fold in the ground almonds and almond extract. Sift in the flour and salt and fold in. Lastly, fold in the apricots. Spoon the mixture into the prepared cake tins and smooth the top with a palette knife or a wooden spoon.

Bake in the oven for about 1 hour, then test with a skewer — if it comes out clean, without batter, the cakes are cooked, otherwise leave them in for another 5—10 minutes. If they start to brown, turn the oven down to 150°C/gas 3.

Take the cakes out of the oven and allow them to cool in the tins. Then remove them to a wire rack and take off the baking paper. Carefully cut each cake in half horizontally, so that you have four layers of sponge.

CONTINUES PAGE 95 ›

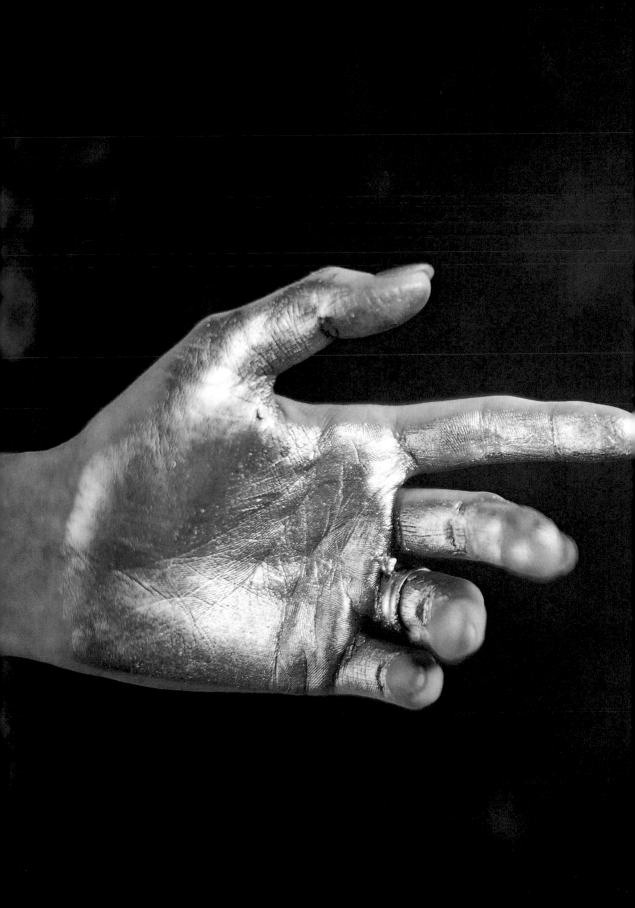

To decorate:
· **1kg white fondant icing**
· **2 tbsp liquid glucose**
· **a couple of packets of Fruity Confetti baking sprinkles**
· **edible metallic gold food paint (we used Rainbow Dust edible silk, in Metallic Gold Treasure)**
· **a splash of vodka**
· **edible origami foxes (see page 192)**

Equipment:
· **a thick clean paintbrush**

To make the filling:
Whip the double cream with 3 tablespoons of icing sugar until soft peaks are formed. Place your first piece of sponge on a flat baking tray. Spread apricot jam over the base, then spread over a nice layer of whipped cream and sprinkle with toasted flaked almonds, which will give a lovely crunch. Repeat with the next two layers, then put the fourth sponge on top, leaving it plain and flat.

To ice the cake:
Put the cake into the fridge to firm up, while you work on your fondant. Dust your work surface with loads of icing sugar, and knead your fondant icing until it is really smooth and soft. Now roll it out to about 0.5cm in thickness.

Remove the cake from the fridge and carefully drape the rolled-out icing over the top of your cake, using the rolling pin if needed. Quickly mould the fondant against the sides, using upward smoothing motions, until it completely covers the cake. Trim off the excess using a small palette knife or sharp knife. Brush the entire cake with the liquid glucose, then grab small handfuls of baking sprinkles and firmly press them all over the fondant.

To bling it up:
Mix the edible metallic gold food paint with a small splash of vodka and stir with a paintbrush. Carefully dab and paint the whole of the cake with gold. It's essential that you dab, not brush.

Top with an edible origami fox or other animal of your choice (see page 192). Stand back and admire!

RAINBOW BATTENBURG CAKE

For the basic sponge:
· 400g unsalted butter, softened
· 400g caster sugar
· 8 free-range eggs
· 400g self-raising Flour
· 300g ground almonds
· ½ tsp baking powder
· 1 tsp almond extract
· milk to loosen

To colour:
· pink food colouring (we use Sugarflair Hollyberry/Pink)
· orange food colouring (we use Sugarflair Apricot)
· yellow food colouring (we use Sugarflair Melon)
· green food colouring (we use Sugarflair Party Green)
· blue food colouring (we use Sugarflair Royal Blue)
· purple food colouring (we use Sugarflair Grape/Violet)

To assemble:
· 200g apricot jam
· 500g block of marzipan
· Icing sugar for dusting

This is a twist on one of our favourite cakes. Traditionally it's just pink and yellow, but the rainbow version looks so impressive and it tastes incredible.

To line the tin:
So that you don't need to buy loads of specialist tins, we're going to tell you how to divide a baking tin into separate sections with tin foil. You're going to line your tin with foil, at the same time cleverly creating the partitions for your rainbow colours!

First grease your tin with butter or margarine, then take a piece of foil double the length of your tin. Press the end of the foil into the end of the tin, then widthways pleat the foil (leaving a 4cm gap from the edge of the tray to make the first section) and mould the foil into the side edges (so that it stands up on its own). Repeat this until your tray has nine separate sections roughly 4cm across (see diagram).

Thoroughly grease the foil all over (including up the sides — you don't want your cake to stick!). Now cut nine strips of greaseproof paper (each 4cm wide) and place one in each section so that the base is covered. Phew! Now that is all done, on to the cake.

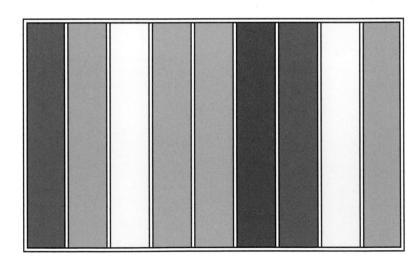

CONTINUES OVERLEAF ›

To watercolour:
· **20ml vodka**
· **food colouring gel of your choice (we have used pink, yellow and green)**
· **muslin cloth**

Equipment:
· **a rectangular baking tin (40cm x 27cm x 2.5cm)**
· **tin foil**
· **rolling pin**

To make the cake:
Preheat your oven to 170°C/gas 5.

Whisk the butter and sugar in a very large bowl with an electric whisk until light and fluffy. Add your eggs one at a time, whisking continuously. Then fold in the flour, ground almonds, baking powder, and almond extract. Add a splash of milk to loosen the mixture if needed.

Divide your mixture evenly between nine bowls. Colour each bowl of mixture with one of your six different food colourings, doubling up on three of the colours — we chose to repeat pink, yellow and orange, but the rainbow combo is up to you! Make sure the batter is very intense in colour, as it will fade during baking.

Carefully fill the sections, and bake for 25–30 minutes — when you insert a skewer, it should come out clean. Allow to cool in the tins for 10 minutes, then transfer to wire racks to finish cooling.

To assemble:
You should now have nine long colourful cake blocks. Trim off any dark edges, and make sure they are all equal in size.

Heat the jam in a small pan until runny, then sieve.

On a surface lightly dusted with icing sugar, roll out the marzipan to roughly 40cm x 30cm and 0.5cm thick.

Use a pastry brush to paint jam all over the sides of each length of sponge.

Place one pink, one orange and one yellow sponge side by side on the 30cm edge of the marzipan, leaving a 4cm gap between the sponge and the 40cm edge. The flap of bare marzipan formed will later be folded over to secure the 40cm edges to each other.

Brush the top of the sponge with more jam, then layer one green, one blue and one purple sponge on top, brushing jam in between to help them stick. Now stick the final three sponges on top, pink, orange and yellow, again brushing jam in between. Smother the whole of the marzipan with jam, then fold the 4cm marzipan flap up, and secure it to the sponge.

CONTINUES OVERLEAF ›

Carefully lift up the rest of the marzipan and smooth it over the cake with your hands, squishing it together and moulding it squarely around the corners, so that it is nice and tight. Connect the other edge of the marzipan to the very corner of the 4cm flap and cut off any excess. Once it's all connected, carefully mould and tweak with your hand to form a perfect rectangular prism. Trim both ends of the cake, using a sharp serrated knife to reveal a clean rainbow Battenberg (those cut-off bits are chef's treats).

To watercolour
Dip one end of your muslin cloth first into the vodka and then into a small amount of food colouring. Test it by dabbing it on a bit of marzipan scrap until you have a lovely shade. Simply dab all over the marzipan, and repeat with the other colours.

If you have any trimmings of sponge left over, you can freeze them and use them for a rainbow-layered trifle.

ETON MESS LAYER CAKE

SERVES 12

For the meringues:
· 1 batch of Meringue
  Girls Mixture (see page 204)
· pink food colouring
  (unnatural: Wilton gel or
  Sugarflair paste/natural:
  Lakeland. Use the Wilton
  gel sparingly or it may
  affect the taste)

For the sponge:
· 400g softened unsalted
  butter
· 400g caster sugar
· 8 eggs
· 400g self-raising flour
· ½ tsp baking powder
· 2 tbsp whole milk
· 2 tsp vanilla bean paste
  (to make your own, see
  page 52)

For the coulis:
· 375g ripe strawberries,
  stalks removed, chopped
  into small pieces
· 30g caster sugar

For the Eton mess cream:
· 600ml double cream
· 150g fresh raspberries,
  squished to a rough
  pulp with a fork
· 2 tbsp fresh mint, finely
  chopped

This is one of our signature cakes. Moist, spongy, creamy, crunchy, tart, meringue-y goodness. Layers of Victoria sponge, sandwiched with Eton mess cream, topped with kisses, glitter-dipped raspberries, fresh mint sprigs and pipettes of coulis, to drizzle and drip.

To make the meringues:
First make your Meringue Girls Mixture. We made some pink kisses and some white kisses (see page 207 for colouring and piping). Pipe meringue kisses of various sizes, little to large, on to a tray lined with baking paper — don't worry if they aren't all perfect, as you can crush the imperfect ones for your Eton mess cream!

Preheat your oven to 100°C/gas ½.

Cook for 30—40 minutes, until the kisses lift off the paper easily. Once cooled, keep the best-looking ones for decoration, and crush up the rest. The meringues keep well for 1 week in a biscuit tin.

To make the cake:
Turn your oven to 160°C/gas 4. Grease two 18cm round cake tins and line with non-stick baking paper.

In a large bowl, beat the butter and sugar together. Add the eggs, one at a time. The mixture may start to look split, but don't worry. Add the flour, baking powder, milk and the vanilla bean paste and beat together until you have a smooth, soft batter.

Divide the mixture between the two tins, smooth the surface with a spatula or the back of a spoon, and bake for about 45 minutes, until golden and the cakes spring back when pressed. Turn them out on to a wire rack and leave to cool completely. Once cool, cut the cakes in half horizontally, so that you have four layers. You can bake, cool and clingfilm the sponges the day before you want to assemble the cake.

To make the coulis:
Put the fresh strawberries and sugar into a pan over a gentle heat. Simmer for 10 minutes, until the fruit breaks down. Push through a sieve using the back of a spoon, and set aside to cool completely. You can make this up to 2 days in advance.

CONTINUES OVERLEAF ›

To decorate:
- a handful of pink and
  white meringue kisses,
  any size
- freeze-dried strawberry
  or raspberry pieces, to
  sprinkle
- mint sprigs
- a handful of fresh
  raspberries
- edible glitter
- pipettes (optional, see
  suppliers, page 221)

To make the Eton mess cream:

Using a stand mixer, or a large mixing bowl and an electric whisk, beat the cream until medium peaks are formed. Set aside a small bowl of the whipped cream for the finishing icing. Place some of the strawberry coulis aside in a separate bowl for the decoration. Swirl the remaining coulis carefully into your bowl of cream. Fold in the crushed meringues, the squished fresh raspberries and the chopped mint, so that everything is just mixed and tastes delicious. (If you want to use a pipette to do the decoration (see below) or to serve with slices of your cake, fill these up now with some of the coulis you set aside.)

To assemble:

Place a layer of sponge on your serving plate and spread a layer of Eton mess cream over the top. Repeat with the rest of the sponges and cream.

To ice the cake, use a palette knife to spread a very thin layer of your reserved whipped cream all over the sides of the cake — so that it is 'semi-naked' and the lovely layers can still be seen. Spread a thicker layer of cream on top.

Arrange some whole meringue kisses around the edge in the shape of a crescent, then scatter with crushed meringues, sprinklings of freeze-dried raspberry or strawberry pieces, sprigs of fresh mint and whole raspberries dipped in edible glitter.

Drizzle the remaining strawberry coulis over the top of the cake and allow it to drip over the edges. We like to fill a few pipettes with coulis and hand them round so that our guests can drizzle extra coulis over their portion.

Now *that* is a cake and a half!

GIRL POWER CAKE

SERVES 12

For the moist chocolate
fudge cake:
· 75g dark chocolate
· 40g black treacle
· 1 tsp vanilla bean paste
  (to make your own, see
  page 52)
· 175g unsalted butter
· 300g plain flour
· 25g cocoa powder
· 375g golden caster sugar
· 1 tsp sea salt
· 1 tsp bicarbonate of soda
· 2 medium free-range eggs
· 200g natural yoghurt

For the filling:
· 200ml double cream
· 3 tbsp runny honey
· 340g good-quality cherry jam
· 200g dark chocolate (70%),
  finely chopped

We don't know what it is about this cake, but it screams GIRL POWER at us. We are seriously fan-girling over Nikki at the Unbirthday bakery, who inspired us to create this floral masterpiece. The base is a moist chocolate fudge cake, sandwiched with cherry choc ganache, and the light grey icing with flower cascade looks super classy, modern and fresh.

To make the cake:
Preheat the oven to 180°C/gas 6. Grease two 18cm round cake tins and line with non-stick baking paper.

Gently melt the chocolate, treacle, vanilla and butter in a small pan and keep stirring until the chocolate is completely melted. In a large bowl mix together the flour, cocoa, sugar, salt and bicarbonate of soda. In a separate bowl whisk the eggs and yoghurt together. Pour the chocolate mixture, egg mixture and 50ml of boiling water into the dry ingredients and gently fold through.

Spoon into the cake tins and bake for 35—40 minutes, until a skewer comes out clean. Leave the cakes to cool in the tins and turn them out on to a wire rack before icing.

To make the filling:
Put the double cream, runny honey and jam into a heavy-based saucepan over a medium heat. As soon as it's begun to simmer, take off the heat immediately and add the dark chocolate. Stir quite vigorously with a wooden spoon, until you have a lovely cherry chocolate ganache. The mixture should be a spreadable consistency. Add a splash of milk if it's too thick.

To make the icing:
Beat the butter using a stand mixer or hand-held electric whisk until pale and almost off-white. Sift in the icing sugar and mix on a low speed until it's incorporated, then add the milk and vanilla and increase the speed until you have a smooth and spreadable buttercream. Now you need to divide your icing up to make the grey icing and purple buttercream stars. For the icing, take three-quarters of the mixture and add the black food colouring, small amounts at a time, until you have an über-cool light grey icing. Add a touch of purple food colouring to the remaining quarter of the icing for making your stars.

CONTINUES OVERLEAF ›

For the icing:
· **250g unsalted butter,
  at room temperature**
· **500g icing sugar**
· **2 tbsp whole milk**
· **1 tsp vanilla bean paste
  (to make your own, see
  page 52)**
· **edible black food colour (we
  use Sugarflair colour paste
  in Black Extra, see suppliers,
  page 220) – you want enough
  to make a light grey colour,
  around ½ tsp**
· **edible purple food colouring
  (we use Sugarflair colour
  paste in Grape/Violet)**

To decorate:
· **fresh flowers (our
  favourite edible flower
  supplier is Greens of Devon,
  see suppliers, page 220;
  however, if you'd like to use
  non-edible flowers, like our
  all-time favourite, rainbow
  roses, be sure to clingfilm
  the stems before sticking
  them into the cake)**
· **a star piping nozzle (we
  used a Wilton no.32 nozzle)**

To assemble:
Cut each cake in half horizontally, so that you have four layers. Stack them up, layer by layer, with your jammy ganache filling. Do not put any on the top.

Cover the entire cake with the grey icing, sides and all. Smooth out the icing with a palette knife so you have a beautiful tall slick cake. Place the purple icing in a piping bag fitted with a star nozzle.

Cascade your chosen flowers down the front of your cake, starting with the largest, then dot the smaller flowers around the edges. Pipe on some purple buttercream stars to add to your gorgeous cascading flower effect.

GIRL POWER!

FAIRY FLOSS CAKE

SERVES 12

For the cake:
· 400g unsalted butter, slightly softened
· 400g caster sugar
· 8 eggs
· 400g self-raising flour
· 75ml whole milk
· zest of 2 unwaxed lemons
· 180g raspberries (frozen work well, but fresh are delish)

For the buttercream base:
· 280g unsalted butter
· 560g icing sugar
· 3–4 tbsp milk

For the yellow buttercream:
· 2 tbsp good-quality lemon curd (we like Waitrose Seriously Zesty)
· yellow food colouring (we used Sugarflair colour paste in Melon)

For the pink buttercream:
· a handful of fresh raspberries, squished
· pink food colouring (we used Sugarflair colour paste in Hollyberry/Pink)

This lemon and raspberry cake is citrusy, sour and sweet. We've decorated it with Pashmak Persian fairy floss, which is made from sesame and sugar, and is a revelation for us – it comes in loads of lovely flavours like pistachio, orange blossom, rose and saffron. It's a wonderful thing to decorate with. Trifles, Eton mess and cakes will always have room for a little fairy floss.

The ombré buttercream smears give a stunning finish to your cake. It's a rough and ready sort of look – just using a palette knife to paste on pink and yellow streaks that merge into each other naturally.

To make the lemon and raspberry sponges:
Preheat the oven to 180°C/gas 6 and line the base of two 18cm cake tins with baking paper, greasing the sides with butter.

Beat the butter and sugar in a large bowl until pale and fluffy. Add the eggs one at a time, scraping the sides of the bowl to make sure everything is well mixed. Sift in the flour, then fold in the milk, lemon zest and raspberries. Be careful not to over-mix the batter — you want to keep it as light, fluffy and airy as possible.

Divide the mixture evenly between the prepared cake tins and smooth over with a palette knife. Bake in the oven for 30—40 minutes, until golden-brown and springy, then leave to cool for about 15 minutes before turning out on to a wire rack to cool completely.

To make the buttercream:
Using a hand-held whisk, electric whisk or stand mixer, whip the butter and icing sugar together until they are light and fluffy, adding milk to loosen. You want your buttercream to be spreadable but firm.

Divide the buttercream between two bowls. To one bowl, add the lemon curd and yellow colouring to give a lovely lemony pastel yellow shade. To the other bowl add a handful of squished raspberries and pink colouring to give a bright pink. Don't mix completely — that way it has a nice marbled effect.

CONTINUES OVERLEAF ›

To assemble:
Layer the sponges using your lemon and raspberry buttercream alternately, plus any extra lemon curd.

To ice, use a palette knife to spread thick smears of pink and yellow icing randomly all over the outside of the cake. Make sure you clean your palette knife in between scooping the buttercream. Decorate with fairy floss in the centre and surround with pink and yellow ombré chocolate discs.

Dim the lights and bring out the sparklers!

To decorate:
- **Pashmak Persian fairy floss (can be bought from Harvey Nichols), or regular fairground candy floss (from Ocado)**
- **yellow and pink ombré chocolate discs (see below)**
- **indoor sparklers**

MAKES 24

- **200g high-quality white chocolate, chopped into very small pieces, or use tempered white chocolate drops or candy melts which don't need to be tempered if you are in a hurry**
- **oil-based food colouring (Wilton works well, but use sparingly or it could affect the taste)**

Equipment:
- **a 24-hole silicone mini muffin tin**

OMBRÉ CHOCOLATE DISCS

These little chocolate discs finish off the cake beautifully. They also look fabulous lined up in a box as a gift.

First you need to temper your white chocolate (see page 216). Working very quickly, add touches of colour to the mix. Fill a few moulds about 0.5cm thick with this paler chocolate, then gradually add more colouring to the bowl of chocolate and as you proceed fill a few more moulds with each shade to build up the ombré effect. Leave to set at room temperature, then pop the chocolates out of the bases.

Package up in an ombré fade in cellophane sweetie bags, or line them up on top of a cake.

THE MOTHER OF ALL CARROT CAKES

SERVES 12

For the cake:
- 215g cooked carrots, puréed to a pulp (see method)
- 1 x 435g tin of pineapple pieces
- 240g plain flour
- 1 tbsp ground cinnamon
- 1 tsp mixed spice
- ½ tsp ground ginger
- ½ tsp ground nutmeg
- 1 tsp table salt
- ½ tbsp bicarbonate of soda
- 210ml vegetable oil
- 3 medium free-range eggs, lightly beaten
- zest of 1 orange
- 380g soft light brown sugar
- 1 tbsp vanilla bean paste
- 75g desiccated coconut
- 100g chopped walnuts, toasted

This really is the mother of all carrot cakes! We are letting you in on a little secret here –cooking the carrot, instead of just grating it, gives such a moist sponge. Yes, yes, we know everyone hates using that word... but moist is the only way to describe it. This masterpiece is decorated with torched Italian meringue icing and daisies.

To make the cake:
There is no need to peel your carrots, just cut them into medium chunks, get rid of the stalks and boil them in water for 15–20 minutes until soft. Drain the carrots in a colander, then put them, along with your pineapple chunks, juice and all, into a blender and whiz to a fine purée. Leave to cool.

Preheat the oven to 170°C/gas 5. Line the base of two 18cm round cake tins with baking paper and grease the sides with a little butter.

Sift the flour, spices, salt and bicarbonate of soda into a medium bowl. In a separate, larger bowl, mix the oil, eggs, orange zest, sugar, puréed carrot and pineapple, vanilla, desiccated coconut and chopped walnuts until very well combined. Gently fold the dry ingredients into the wet ingredients until just combined.

Divide the mixture evenly between the prepared cake tins, and bake for 40–50 minutes, until a skewer comes out clean. Let the cakes cool in the tins, then loosen the sides with a knife and pop them out on to a wire rack to cool completely. Cut each cake in half horizontally, so that you have four layers. If you are doing this in advance, clingfilm them until ready to use.

To make the filling:
Make the limey cream cheese filling for between the layers by mixing together the mascarpone, cream cheese, icing sugar and lime zest and juice until you have a smooth thick icing. You can do this up to 2 days in advance.

CONTINUES OVERLEAF ›

**For the mascarpone
lime filling:**
· 200g mascarpone cheese
· 400g full-fat cream cheese
· 170g icing sugar, sifted
· zest and juice of 2 limes

For the icing:
· 1 batch of Italian
  meringue (see page 215)

To decorate:
· fresh edible white flowers

To assemble:
Make your Italian meringue.

Place one layer of carrot cake on a lovely cake stand or platter. Spread it with a layer of the limey cream cheese filling and sandwich with another layer of cake. Continue until all four layers are stacked up. Do not put any filling on the top.

Using a palette knife, spread a rustic layer of Italian meringue around all the sides and top of the cake. Then gently toast with a blowtorch, until the meringue turns a beautiful deep golden colour. Dot flowers all over the cake.

Your mother would be proud.

BOOM TING
JAFFA CAKES

MAKES 12

For the Jaffa cake bases
· 150g whole boiled
  blended oranges (approx.
  1½ oranges) (see method)
· 2 medium free-range eggs
· 95g caster sugar
· 95g ground almonds
· ¼ tsp gluten-free baking
  powder
· ⅛ tsp gluten-free
  bicarbonate of soda
· 60g of marmalade, about
  1 tsp per Jaffa cake

For the orange jelly:
· 1 x 135g packet of
  orange jelly
· zest of 1 orange

For the chocolate coating:
· 100g 70% dark chocolate
  broken into squares
· ½ tsp orange extract

Equipment:
· 12 hole muffin tin

We could eat a whole box of Jaffa cakes in one sitting... easily. We really do love them, but often they are stale-bottomed, with far too little orange jelly.

This is a super pimped-out Jaffa cake recipe that uses an incredible orange and almond cake base – it's dairy free and gluten free, with no oil or butter. Just boiled oranges, blended with the skin on, which gives the cake moisture. And just imagine topping these incredible bases with thick and tangy orange jelly, then covering them in rich dark chocolate. Full moon, half moon... total eclipse!

To make the cakes:
Put the oranges into a pan and cover them with cold water. Bring to the boil and cook on a high heat for 30—45 minutes, until very soft throughout when pierced with a knife. Drain and leave to cool. Now halve the oranges, remove any pips, and blitz in a food processor or with a hand-held stick blender, skin and all, until very smooth. Leave to cool completely. You can do this up to 3 days in advance and keep the orange purée in the fridge, or freeze it for up to a month, until you are ready to use. Great if you have oranges nearly going off in the fruit bowl.

Preheat the oven to 180°C/gas 6. Prepare a 12-hole muffin tin. A silicone one is best, as you don't need to grease it — if you are using a metal tin, you need to grease each hole and line the base with a circle of baking paper.

In a large bowl, thoroughly mix together the eggs, caster sugar, ground almonds and blitzed oranges. Gently fold in the baking powder and bicarbonate of soda.

Fill each muffin hole a quarter of the way up with the mixture. Bake in the oven for 15—20 minutes, until the cakes have risen and are springy to the touch. Leave to cool until they are stable enough to pop out of the moulds, then put on a wire rack to cool completely.

To make the jelly:
Follow the instructions on the packet, using 20ml less water than the amount stated, and adding the zest of 1 orange. Line a 12-hole muffin tin with clingfilm, and pour in the jelly mixture so that it is about 1cm thick. Refrigerate until firm. >

CONTINUES OVERLEAF ›

To assemble:
Spread a little marmalade on top of each cake, so that the jelly discs will stick. When the jelly is completely set, carefully pull out the clingfilm to release the discs and flip a jelly on top of each cake.

To finish, melt the chocolate in a microwave or in a glass bowl over a saucepan of boiling water, making sure the bottom of the bowl does not touch the water. Stir the chocolate until melted and add ½ teaspoon of orange extract. Let the chocolate cool right down, as it will melt the jelly if it's too hot.

Put some baking paper under the wire rack to catch the chocolatey drips, then spoon the melted chocolate over the orange jelly. Put into the fridge immediately and leave to set.

LIME AND BLUEBERRY POLENTA PYRAMIDS

MAKES 6

For the blueberry compote:
· 50g blueberries
· 15g caster sugar

For the lime and blueberry polenta cake:
· 60g unsalted butter, softened
· 75g caster sugar
· 1 large free-range egg, at room temperature
· 60g ground almonds
· 35g fine polenta
· ¼ tsp gluten-free baking powder
· 50g blueberries
· zest and juice of 1 lime
· a little pinch of salt

For the lime drizzle:
· juice of 1 lime
· 50g icing sugar

Optional decorations:
· fresh blueberries
· flaked almonds, toasted
· edible gold leaf

Equipment:
· a 6-hole pyramid silcone mould (we bought ours from Nisbets, see suppliers, page 221)

This is a delicious gluten-free cake recipe. We first saw these moulds being used by a really cute local baker – Laura from Hackney Yolk. These pyramid moulds are a gorgeous shape for mini bakes, which are so much more unusual than a standard cupcake, but just as easy.

To make the compote:
Place the blueberries and sugar in a heavy-based saucepan with ½ tablespoon of water and slowly bring to the boil, stirring all the time with a wooden spoon. Once all the berries have broken down and become soft (after about 10 minutes), push them through a sieve into a bowl, using the back of a spoon. Leave to cool.

To make the cake:
Preheat the oven to 170°C/gas 5. Grease the holes in the silicone baking mould with butter.

Using a stand mixer, or a bowl and a hand-held whisk, mix the butter and sugar until pale and fluffy. Add the egg and combine until well incorporated. Now fold in your almonds, polenta, baking powder, blueberries, lime zest, juice and salt — do not over-mix, otherwise the crumb will be dense. Spoon a teaspoon of blueberry compote into each hole in the pyramid mould (keeping the rest for later), followed by the cake mix (until it reaches about three-quarters of the way up). Place the pyramid mould on a baking tray and bake for 25—30 minutes, until a skewer or cocktail stick comes out clean.

To make the lime drizzle:
Slowly mix the lime juice into the icing sugar until you have a smooth drizzly consistency.

To assemble:
Once the pyramids are baked, leave them to cool slightly in the moulds for about 10 minutes, then turn them out on to a wire cooling rack and drizzle with your lime icing. Top with the remaining blueberry compote, and some flaked almonds — we added a final finishing touch with a fresh blueberry topped with gold leaf.

IT'S ALL ABOUT THE COCONUT FLOUR BROWNIES

MAKES 16

· 250g unsalted butter, melted
· 200g dark chocolate
  (at least 70%), cut into
  very small pieces
· 70g coconut flour
· 1 tsp gluten-free baking
  powder
· 1 tsp sea salt for the
  mixture, plus a little
  extra to sprinkle on top
· 80g cocoa powder
  (at least 70%)
· 4 large free-range eggs
· 360g caster sugar
· 100g pistachios, chopped,
  a mixture of fine and
  coarse chunks

Equipment:
· 20cm Square Baking Tin

The gorgeous Chloe from Fatties Bakery introduced us to these beauties when we first met. They are the squidgiest, most delicious brownies you will ever eat, and the best thing about them is that they are gluten free. It's all about the coconut flour! This will be your go-to brownie recipe, like, for ever...

Heat your oven to 180°C/gas 6. Prepare a 20cm square baking tin with a little oil and non-stick baking paper.

Melt the butter in a saucepan over a medium heat, stirring gently. Once completely melted, remove from the heat and add the dark chocolate. Stir until the chocolate melts and the mixture is well combined.

Put the coconut flour, baking powder, salt, and cocoa powder into a large bowl and mix until they're well incorporated.

Place the eggs in the bowl of a stand mixer fitted with a whisk, or use a hand-held electric whisk, and beat until light and creamy. Alternatively you can do this by hand using a bit of elbow grease! Add the sugar and continue to beat until all is incorporated.

Gradually add the melted chocolate and butter mixture to the egg and sugar mixture, whisking the whole time. Gently fold in the coconut flour mixture, making sure everything is well incorporated, but trying not to knock out any air.

Finally fold though most of the pistachios. Spoon into your prepared tin and level out, then sprinkle the rest of the pistachios on top and dust with an extra sprinkle of sea salt.

Bake for about 20 minutes, or until a skewer inserted around the outside of the cake comes out clean. The very middle can still be pretty squidgy — you want to take it out when it's slightly under-baked, so that it stays super-gooey and moist. Cool in the tray before cutting.

For an amazing dessert, serve warm, with a dollop of crème fraîche and a sprinkling of pomegranate seeds!

Ain't no party like an OMG party!

HOMEMADE PEANUT BUTTER CUPS

MAKES 24 MINI CUPS

· 300g good-quality dark chocolate
· 150g smooth peanut butter (or other nut butter, such as cashew or almond)
· 30g icing sugar, sifted
· 1½ tbsp salted butter, softened
· a pinch of sea salt

For the topping:
· a handful of salted peanuts, finely chopped
· a pinch of sea salt

Equipment:
· a 24-hole mini-muffin tin
· mini-muffin paper cases

Peanut butter cups are one of our favourite treats. These are inspired by the super-talented Lotta from Eat Chic, who we share our bakery with – she makes the most amazing PB cups! We love ours made with really bitter dark chocolate, but milk or white work well too. For a break from the norm, why not try using other nut butters? It's so simple to make your own nut butters, too – almond, cashew, pecan, hazelnut, homemade Nutella. The higher the fat in the nut, the smoother the butter will be. If you fancy giving this a go, see page 33.

Start by lining your mini-muffin tin with your paper cases.

Now temper your dark chocolate — go on, try it, it's simple if you just stick to the three temperatures on page 216, and it will make such a lovely professional peanut butter cup with a great snap when you bite into it. If you need a quick PB fix to munch now, just gently melt your chocolate in a glass bowl over a bain-marie or in the microwave. It will still taste amazing.

Pour a touch of the melted choc into all 24 cases, so it barely covers the bottom — you just want to create a thin shell. Use a clean finger to spread the chocolate all the way up the sides, so it coats the cases. Leave to set at room temperature for 10 minutes.

While you're waiting, beat your chosen nut butter, icing sugar, butter and salt together with a wooden spoon so that it's nice and creamy. Place a teaspoon of nut butter filling into each muffin case, then gently pat down flat with your fingers and set aside.

You may need to quickly reheat your chocolate to get it liquid again. It shouldn't go out of temper if you blast it for a couple of seconds in the microwave to just a couple of degrees higher, or pop it back over the saucepan of simmering water for a minute.

Once melted again, use a teaspoon to pour chocolate over the top of the cups until the nut butter is completely covered, tapping the muffin tin gently on your work surface repeatedly to ensure a nice flat top.

Sprinkle the chopped peanuts over the top of each cup, and leave somewhere cool to set completely. Finally, sprinkle with sea salt before serving. Remember, if you've tempered your chocolate, don't leave it to set in the fridge or it will lose its shine.

MINT CHOC ICE CREAM MERINGUE SANDWICHES

MAKES 6

For the meringue sandwiches:
· 1 batch of Meringue Girls Mixture (see page 204)
· a couple of drops of green food colouring (unnatural: Wilton gel or Sugarflair paste/natural: Lakeland. Use Wilton gel sparingly or it can affect the taste)
· 100g dark chocolate chips
· 50g ground almonds
· 1 tsp white wine vinegar
· 3 drops of peppermint extract

For the filling:
· 1 x 500ml tub of mint choc chip ice cream

Mint and chocolate are a classic combo for a reason . . . they take you to tastebud heaven. There's nothing quite like the crunchy, chewy, creamy texture of a meringue ice cream sandwich. There's only one problem (which isn't really a problem . . .) – you have to devour them as fast as possible before they melt.

First make your Meringue Girls Mixture. Then carefully fold a few drops of green food colouring, the chocolate chips, almonds, vinegar and peppermint extract into the meringue mixture until just combined. Try not to knock out all the air you have just created.

Preheat the oven to 100°C/gas ½.

Spoon 1 heaped tablespoonful of meringue at a time on to two lined A4-sized flat baking trays, and gently smooth out to form flat oval discs about 8cm long, 5cm wide and 1cm thick. Make sure you leave at least 1cm between the discs, as they will expand a little in the oven.

Bake for about 35–40 minutes, or until they lift off the baking paper easily. Set aside to cool.

Now you are ready to sandwich your sandwiches! To serve, spoon a big tablespoonful of ice cream between two meringue halves and gently squish between your hands. Ready, steady, scoff.

BANANA POPS

MAKES 4

· 2 fresh bananas
· 100g good-quality dark
  chocolate (sea salt
  flavour works well, or
  add a pinch of sea salt)
· 1 tsp coconut oil (sold in
  healthfood shops – it is
  solid in the jar)

Your choice of toppings:
· roasted pistachios,
  roughly chopped
· toasted walnuts, roughly
  chopped
· dried rose petals
· freeze-dried raspberries
· toasted flaked almonds
· coconut flakes
· whole Oreo biscuits, crushed

Equipment:
· 4 lollypop sticks

These are a delicious guilt-free summer treat, and the perfect 'DIY' party activity. Pull your ready-frozen bananas out of the freezer and dip them in melted chocolate and toppings. The (big) kids absolutely love it, and they are a deceptively healthy snack.

Peel your bananas and cut them in half. Pop a lollypop stick in the base of each. Put them on a lined baking tray and chill in the freezer for at least 4 hours (best overnight), to harden up ready for dipping.

Roughly chop your chocolate bar and put it into a heatproof bowl with 1 teaspoon of coconut oil. Gently melt together in a microwave or over a pan of boiling water. Adding the coconut oil to the chocolate gives you that lovely old-school cracked shell effect over the banana once it's frozen.

Dip the frozen bananas in the melted chocolate, then sprinkle with your chosen toppings. Freeze again for 30–45 minutes, until hard.

Now get chomping.

STRAW-BRÛLÉE

MAKES ABOUT 40

· ½ batch of Italian Meringue
  (see page 215)
· 2 punnets of fresh
  strawberries

Equipment:
· a blowtorch

A really simple idea, but one that is super delicious and perfect for a lil' party. Either serve ready brûléed on trays, or let your guests dip and toast at the end of a meal for a real 'Come Dine With Me' experience.

You can make your Italian meringue up to 24 hours before you want to serve your guests. As the hot sugar syrup partially cooks the egg whites it is a very stable mixture — so will happily sit in the fridge in a clingfilmed bowl until you are ready to dip your strawberries.

1. Hold the strawberries by their stalks.
2. Generously dip into the Italian meringue.
3. Use a blowtorch to lightly toast the meringue.
4. Pop into your mouth.

TITANIC ICEBERGS

MAKES 4

For the meringue iceberg:
· **1 batch of Meringue Girls Mixture (see page 204)**
· **1 vanilla pod**

For the hot chocolate (you can swap with a coffee if you prefer):
· **900ml milk**
· **175ml double cream**
· **225g milk or dark chocolate, broken into squares**

A vanilla bean meringue iceberg floating on a rich creamy hot chocolate. Curl up by the roaring fire, don your Heart of the Ocean necklace, dig out your Celine Dion playlist, and daydream of snogging Leo.

To make the meringue icebergs:
Make your Meringue Girls Mixture. Split your vanilla pod in half and scrape out the seeds, then gently fold them through the stiff meringue mixture.

Preheat the oven to 100°C/gas ½. Line a flat baking tray with baking paper. Draw circles on your baking paper, a third smaller than the rim of your coffee cups. You want the final iceberg to float on the hot chocolate and fill the whole cup, and the meringue will expand during baking so you need to allow for growth.

Spoon the meringue into a disposable piping bag and cut a hole the size of a 5p coin in the tip of the bag. Pipe your icebergs on to the baking paper within the drawn circles — for each start with a big dome shape, then build up the iceberg with spikes.

Bake for 2 hours, until they are set and lift off the baking paper cleanly. Store in a biscuit tin for up to 2 weeks, or until you are ready to set sail on your daydream.

To make the hot chocolate:
Put the milk and cream into a small heavy-based saucepan and bring to a gentle simmer over a low heat. Add the chocolate squares to your mugs, pour over the hot milk and cream and stir until the chocolate has completely melted. Top with your big white icebergs, and serve . . . but don't let go!

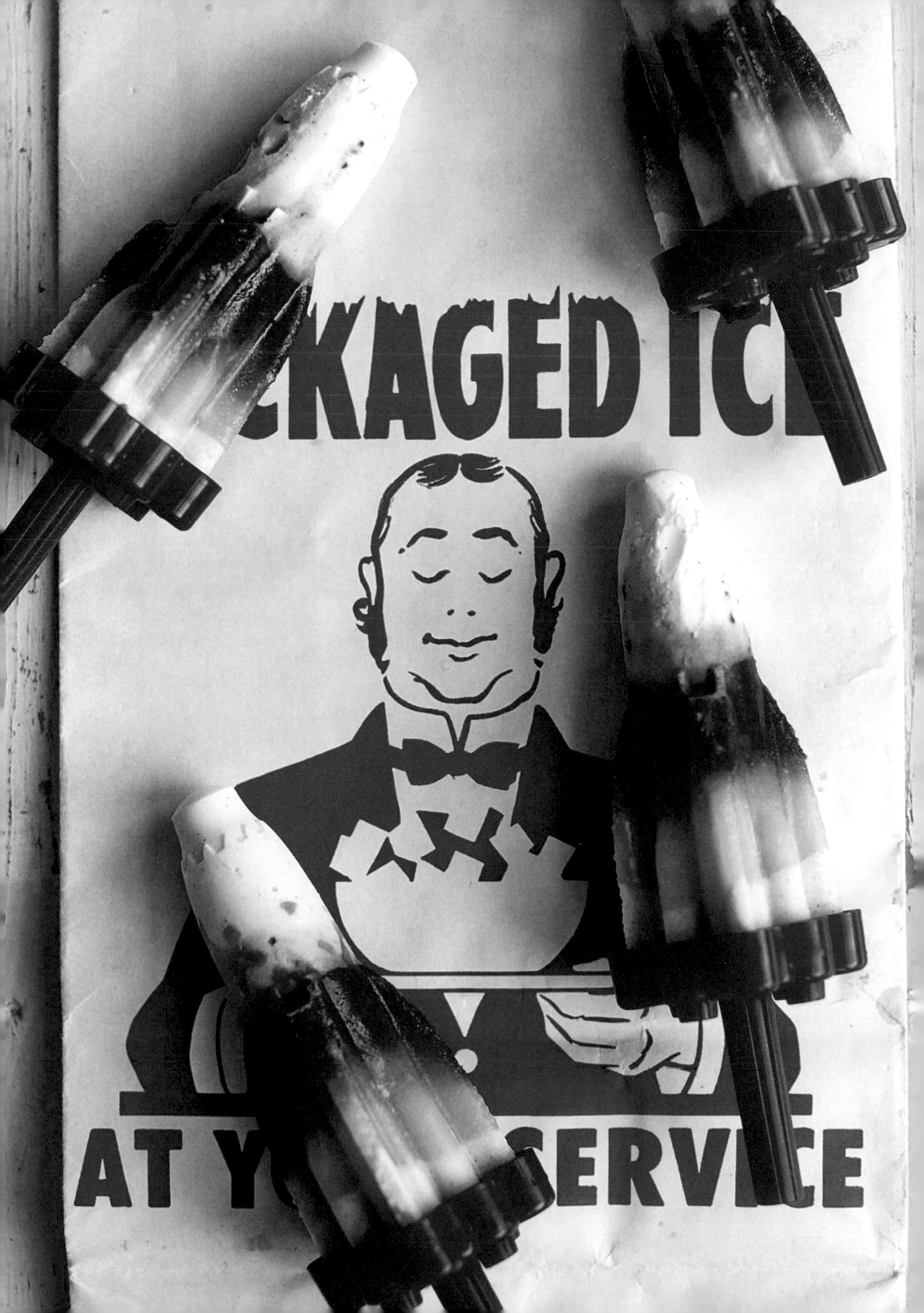
CKAGED IC
AT Y
SERVICE

COYO, MANGO AND RASPBERRY ROCKETS

MAKES 4

· 125g fresh raspberries
· 4 tbsp agave syrup (if you
  don't have this, honey
  will work nicely too)
· 1 vanilla pod
· 200g coconut yoghurt
· 1 small ripe mango,
  destoned and peeled

Equipment:
· 4 ice lolly moulds
· 4 lollipop sticks

These little beauties are the perfect treat on a hot summer's day and are incredibly easy to make. The creaminess of the coconut yoghurt works so well with the tart mango and raspberry coulis. They are dairy free, gluten free and you wouldn't even know it...

Put the raspberries into a small bowl with 2 tablespoons of agave syrup and crush until the berries have turned to mush.

Split the vanilla pod in half and scrape the seeds into a bowl. Add the coyo yoghurt and 1 tablespoon of agave syrup, whisk until smooth and put to one side.

In a food processor, blend the mango with the remaining tablespoon of agave syrup.

You've now got two options:

For the speedy option:
For a creamy pop, swirl everything together and divide the mixture evenly between the 4 moulds. Transfer to the freezer. Pop your lollipop sticks in after 30 minutes, then leave for 4 hours to set completely.

For the long-winded but beautiful option:
For a layered pop, pour one third of the coyo into your four lolly moulds and freeze for 10 minutes. Put half of the remaining coyo into a bowl, mix in half the mango pulp, then pour into the moulds and freeze for another 10 minutes. Now pour the rest of the mango pulp into the moulds and freeze for a further 10 minutes. Mix half the raspberries into your final bit of coyo and pour into the moulds. Now, for the final layer, pour in your remaining raspberry mush and freeze for 4 hours, until set completely.

BLACK SESAME ÉCLAIRS

MAKES 12

For the choux pastry:
· 105g plain flour, well sifted
· a pinch of table salt
· 85g butter, cut into small
  pieces to help it melt quickly
· 220ml tap water
· 3 medium free-range
  eggs, beaten

For the crème pâtissière:
· 4 medium free-range
  egg yolks (remember,
  you can always use the
  whites for meringue!)
· 100g caster sugar
· 15g plain flour
· 15g cornflour
· 350ml whole milk
· 2 tbsp black sesame seeds,
  toasted in a dry pan
  to release the flavour,
  and crushed finely in a
  pestle and mortar or spice
  blender

For the glaze:
· fondant icing sugar
· Sugarflair colour paste in
  Black Extra (see suppliers,
  page 220)

If we hadn't gone into the meringue business, the choux game would have been our next choice. We absolutely love the art of pastry-making and this is by far the most fun and most forgiving of all pastries. Black sesame is one of our favourite flavours at the moment, and combined with velvety crème patissiere it's total heaven.

To make the choux pastry:
Sieve the flour and salt into a small bowl.

Place the butter and water in a medium heavy-based pan and heat gently until the butter melts. Then crank up the heat until it's at a rolling boil. When it's boiling furiously, take it off the heat and quickly tip in the flour and salt.

Immediately beat hard with a wooden spoon to get the mixture to form a ball. Once it has JUST come together, stop stirring. The less you stir now, the smoother your éclairs will be — if you overbeat now, they often crack.

Spread the paste on to a dinner plate (don't wash your pan yet, as you can use it later) and let it cool to room temperature — you can do this in the fridge to speed up the process, but don't allow it to get too cold, or it won't absorb enough egg in the next step, and the egg is key to making the éclairs rise when baked.

When the paste is at room temperature, put it back into your pan and vigorously mix in the beaten eggs a little at a time. Slow and steady is key, so that the mixture doesn't split. Keep adding egg until you have a smooth 'dropping' consistency, i.e. it drops off the spoon in a blob — it doesn't just stick to the spoon when you flick, and it doesn't dribble off. You may need a little more or a little less egg.

Now your choux pastry is made! It's such a lovely pastry — it keeps for 3 days in the fridge in an airtight container or piping bag, or can be frozen for up to a month and defrosted when you are ready to use it. Ideal.

To make the éclairs:
Preheat the oven to 200°C/gas 7. Transfer the choux paste to a large piping bag fitted with a 1.5cm round nozzle. Line a large baking tray with greaseproof paper and pipe out 12 éclairs, each about 15cm long.

Bake the éclairs in the preheated oven for 20—25 minutes, or until golden-brown. Remove them from the oven and use a skewer to make a hole the size of a pea in one end of each éclair, then return them to the oven for another

Optional decorations:
· white and black
  sesame seeds
· silver leaf (see suppliers,
  page 220)

Equipment:
· disposable piping bags
· a 1cm nozzle

5 minutes to dry them out in the middle. Leave them to cool on a wire rack.

Another clever trick with choux paste is to pipe out your éclairs and freeze them uncooked. They freeze really well for up to a month. When you are ready to bake, just add 10 more minutes to the cooking time above.

To make the crème patissiere:
In a large mixing bowl, whisk together the yolks and sugar until they turn a pale gold colour. Whisk in the flour and cornflour and set aside. Place the milk and the finely crushed black sesame seeds in a heavy-based saucepan and bring to a gentle simmer, stirring frequently. Remove from the heat and leave to cool for 30 seconds.

Slowly pour half the hot milk on to the cold egg mixture, whisking all the time, then return the mixture to the remaining milk in the pan. Doing it this way prevents the eggs from scrambling. Bring the mixture back to the boil and simmer for 1 minute, whisking continuously until smooth.

Pour the crème pat into a clean bowl and cover with clingfilm. Cool, then refrigerate until needed. It will keep in the fridge for up to 3 days.

To fill the eclairs:
Prepare a disposable piping bag with a 1cm nozzle and fill with your black sesame crème pat. Holding the piping bag tightly with one hand and an éclair with the other, pipe the mixture into the pea size hole until each éclair feels heavy and full.

To make the glaze and decoration:
Place the fondant icing sugar in a bowl and gradually add a few drops of water at a time until you have a smooth, thick, but pipeable fondant. Next add the paste colour (however dark you fancy) with a cocktail stick — the colour is really concentrated, so you don't need much. Mix until the colour looks even, then transfer to a disposable piping bag. Cut a small hole in the end (around 0.5cm), then carefully pipe lines along the length of each éclair — don't worry if they aren't completely straight, as this just adds to their charm!

While the fondant is still sticky, sprinkle the éclairs with black and white sesame seeds. If you want to make them look super glam, add a little silver leaf to each one. Use either a small knife or a dry paintbrush to lift the silver leaf from the packet — be careful not to touch it with your hand or anything damp, otherwise it will really cling to the wrong thing! Transfer from the paintbrush directly to the sticky fondant. Serious wow factor.

CHOCOLATE COOKIEMUFFS

MAKES 24

· 110g unsalted butter, softened (plus extra for greasing)
· 110g light brown sugar
· 110g caster sugar
· 1 egg
· ½ tsp vanilla bean paste, homemade (see page 52) or store-bought
· 220g plain flour
· ½ tsp salt
· ½ tsp bicarbonate of soda
· 300g milk chocolate chips

Equipment:
· a 24-hole mini-muffin tin

Is it a cookie? Is it a muffin? No – it's a cookiemuff! An ooey-gooey melted chocolate centre with a chocolate chip cookie surround. These little cross-breeds are the most indulgent, fudgy toadstools you will ever eat. Perfect Sunday baking.

Preheat the oven to 170°C/gas 5. Lightly grease your mini-muffin tin with butter. If you have a stand mixer, pop your butter and both sugars into it and beat until light and fluffy. Alternatively you can use an electric hand whisk or just good old-fashioned elbow grease.

Add the egg and vanilla and continue to beat until creamy.

Sift together the flour, salt and bicarbonate of soda, then add to the butter and sugar and fold by hand until just combined.

Add half the chocolate chips and give the mixture a good stir to distribute them. Now melt the rest of your chocolate chips in a heatproof bowl in the microwave on a very low setting, stirring every 30 seconds. Alternatively, place the chocolate in a glass bowl over a pan of boiling water, making sure the water does not touch the bottom of the bowl. Keep stirring, and the steam will melt the chocolate.

Make little balls of dough in your hands, and press them down into the muffin holes with your fingers so the mixture comes up the sides a little. Make a little indent with your thumb to hold the melted chocolate. Leave some dough for the toadstool tops.

Using a teaspoon, dollop a little bit of melted chocolate into each indent. Then take little pieces of the reserved cookie dough and place them on top of each one, to create a plug — it doesn't matter if the dough doesn't cover all the melted chocolate, but try to cover as much as possible.

Bake for 15—20 minutes, until the edges are hardened and a little brown and crackled. Take them out when they are still squidgy, as they will harden more while they cool.

Leave to cool slightly in the tin, then use a knife to loosen the edges of each cookiemuff. They are best eaten warm.

To eat later on — ping in the microwave for 20 seconds to re-melt the gooey chocolate middle. Deeeeeeelish.

PROSECCO, STRAWBERRY AND POPPING CANDY TRUFFLES

MAKES 25

For the truffle ganache:
· 280g good-quality dark chocolate (70%)
· 250ml double cream
· 50g unsalted butter
· 100ml Prosecco (drink the rest of the bottle while eating your truffles)

For coating:
· 60g freeze-dried strawberries
· 60g coated popping candy (see suppliers, page 220), or normal 'Fizz Wiz' popping candy

Homemade chocolate truffles are deceptively easy to make, yet so impressive. The perfect little treat for popping in your mouth when you're sitting on the sofa, after dinner, or if you are planning a decadent high tea. Everyone's heard of champagne truffles, but these use our fave fizzy Italian tipple – prosecco.

Line a large baking tray with baking paper.

Start by making the truffle ganache. Break the chocolate into squares and place in a large glass bowl. Heat the cream and butter in a saucepan over a low heat, and stir until the butter is melted. Let the cream reach a gentle simmer, then pour over the chocolate, whisking until it's completely melted. Add the prosecco and whisk until combined. Pour the lot into a lined shallow tin and refrigerate for at least 4 hours, and preferably overnight.

Mix your freeze-dried strawberries and popping candy together on a large plate and set aside.

To shape the truffles, dip a melon baller or teaspoon into a cup of boiling water. Scrape up balls of the ganache, reshaping them with your hands if necessary, then drop them on to the plate of freeze-dried strawberries and popping candy, rolling them around to get an even coverage. Repeat until you've used all the ganache. Place the truffles on a baking tray lined with baking paper and chill in the fridge for about 30 minutes before enjoying.

Coated popping candy doesn't absorb the moisture of the truffles, so the 'POP' stays until you bite into them. Uncoated 'Fizz Wiz' works well, but absorbs the moisture, so these are best eaten quickly. If you prefer to keep your truffles simple, just roll them in good-quality cocoa powder.

INSTANT BANANA I-SCREAM

SERVES 4

For the ice cream:
· 5 ripe bananas, peeled and frozen in small pieces (see method)

Optional toppings:
· toasted coconut shavings
· chopped walnuts
· cocoa nibs
· freeze-dried raspberries
· pistachios
· roasted salted peanuts
· chocolate shavings

I scream, you scream, we all scream for ice cream! This is the easiest recipe ever. Who would have thought that just frozen bananas, whizzed up in a blender, could produce such a rich, creamy and smooth ice cream? It's total magic. We constantly have a stash of frozen bananas in our freezer now, ready to pull out when the mood strikes us. You can happily eat this plain, or add any type of flavouring you want. We have used cocoa and cinnamon, but you could add fresh berries, nuts, or any kind of spice, such as nutmeg or cardamom. Kids would never ever know the difference between this and real ice cream. It's so nourishing you could even have it for breakfast.

Peel the bananas and cut them into 1cm thick rounds. Place them in a sealed bag and freeze for at least 4 hours. It's best to do this the night before, and they can even stay in your freezer for months!

Put your frozen bananas into a strong food processor and blend to a smooth ice cream consistency (it takes about 4 minutes to get from bitty to smooth and creamy).

Serve immediately, sprinkled with delicious toppings of your choice!

Mc G'S FRIED APPLE PIES

MAKES 4

For the pies:
· 4 Bramley apples, peeled, cored and cut into 1cm cubes
· 4 tbsp soft light brown sugar
· a small knob of butter
· 2 tsp ground cinnamon
· 1 tsp freshly grated nutmeg
· 1 packet of pre-rolled puff pastry
· 1 egg, beaten
· 1 litre vegetable oil, for frying

For the coating:
· 2 tbsp icing sugar
· 1 tsp ground cinnamon
· 4 tsp pearl sugar (optional – see suppliers, page 220)
· sea salt

No need to drive all the way to Mc D's! These Mc G bad boys are simple, naughty and incredibly delicious – a hot spiced apple filling in a sugary, cinnamony deep-fried puff pastry case. The stuff of dreams!

Start by stewing your apples. Place them in a heavy-based saucepan on a medium heat and add the sugar, butter, cinnamon and nutmeg. Stir until the butter has melted, then turn down to a simmer, cover the pan and cook for 10 minutes, or until the apples have softened but still hold their shape. Remove from the heat and leave to cool completely.

Unroll your puff pastry sheet. Using a sharp knife, cut it into four long strips. Spoon about 3 teaspoons of your apple mixture on to one half of each strip and fold the other half over lengthways. Dab some beaten egg around the edges with a pastry brush, then use a fork to press grooves around the sides. Refrigerate the pies for at least 15 minutes, to get the pastry very cold, or freeze until you are ready to cook them.

Heat the oil in a wok or a deep, heavy-based saucepan. Being extremely careful, drop a small piece of puff pastry into the oil. If it sizzles and rises to the top within 5 seconds, the oil is hot enough. Be very careful when deep-frying, as the oil can often spit back at you. Fry the pies, two at a time max, for approximately 5–7 minutes, until golden and delicious, gently flipping them for ultimate coverage. Once golden, lift them out using a slotted spoon and leave to drain on kitchen paper, making sure you get rid of any excess oil.

To make the coating, mix the icing sugar and cinnamon in a shallow bowl. While the pies are still warm, coat them generously in the cinnamon sugar, then sprinkle with pearl sugar and a pinch of sea salt and serve immediately.

OUR ULTIMATE BANANA SPLIT WITH 'HOMEMADE' PEANUT BUTTER ICE CREAM

SERVES 4

· **500ml good quality vanilla ice cream**
· **3 heaped tbsp peanut butter (try making your own homemade nut butter, see page 33)**
· **4 bananas**
· **1 tbsp oil, for frying**
· **100g dark chocolate (70%)**
· **100g salted peanuts**

For the salted caramel sauce:
· **100g caster sugar**
· **a knob of butter**
· **60g double cream**
· **a big pinch of sea salt**

The perfect comfort dessert – easy 'homemade' peanut butter ice cream, caramelized bananas, hot toasted peanuts, warm salted caramel sauce and, of course, melted chocolate.

First make your peanut butter ice cream. Combine your ice cream and peanut butter in the bowl of a stand mixer and beat together using the paddle attachment until well combined. Alternatively, do this in a bowl using a wooden spoon or spatula. Taste, add more peanut butter if you want to, then spoon back into your ice cream tub and put back into the freezer to re-harden.

Make your salted caramel sauce by gently heating the caster sugar in a heavy-based pan until it melts into a golden caramel. Quickly and carefully stir in a knob of butter and the double cream until it comes into a lovely creamy caramel. Take off the heat and season with a big pinch of sea salt.

Slit your bananas lengthways, keeping the skins on. Heat the oil in a frying pan on a medium heat and fry the bananas skin side down for a few minutes, until the skins start to go black and translucent. Then flip them over and caramelize the flesh side until nice and golden.

To melt the chocolate, break it into squares and place it in a heatproof bowl over a saucepan of simmering water, making sure the base of the bowl does not touch the water. Alternatively heat it gently in a microwave.

Meanwhile, put the peanuts into a hot pan and toast them slightly. Once they're done, transfer them to a small bowl to stop them cooking.

To assemble, place two pieces of caramelized banana, still with the skin on, in each bowl. Top with two or three scoops of your ice cream, then drizzle over the warm salted caramel sauce, the melted chocolate and finish with a sprinkling of roasted peanuts. Devour immediately!

COCKTAIL O'CLOCK! MOJITO BAKED ALASKAS

MAKES 4

For the mojito sorbet (can also be shop-bought!):
· 125ml fresh lime juice
· 4 tbsp Jamaican white rum
· 150g icing sugar
· 120ml water
· zest of 1 lime
· a handful of mint (roughly 20 leaves), finely sliced

For the sponge:
· 170g softened unsalted butter
· 170g caster sugar
· 3 eggs
· 100g self-raising flour
· 70g desiccated coconut
· juice and zest of 2 limes

For the brown sugar Italian meringue:
· 60g egg whites (from 2 medium eggs)
· 50g caster sugar
· 75g light brown sugar
· 30ml water

Equipment:
· a sugar thermometer
· a blowtorch
· cocktail umbrellas
· 8cm Cookie Cutter

Baked Alaska is an absolute classic meringue recipe. We have given it a Meringue Girls twist by combining a zesty lime and coconut sponge with mojito sorbet and blowtorched brown sugar Italian meringue. A proper summer holiday on a plate. Don't forget your cocktail umbrella!

To make the mojito sorbet:
Put the lime juice, rum and icing sugar into a bowl and whisk until the sugar has dissolved. Stir in the water, lime zest and mint. Pour into an airtight container and freeze overnight. Due to the alcohol content this sorbet doesn't freeze very hard so move fast once you take it out of the freezer.

To make the sponge:
Preheat the oven to 170°C/gas 5. Butter a large baking tin (approximately 24cm x 18cm) and line it with non-stick baking paper.

In a large bowl or using a stand mixer, beat the butter and sugar together until light and fluffy. Add the eggs one at a time — the mixture may start to look split, but don't worry. Add the flour, coconut, lime juice and zest and fold gently until you have a smooth batter. Pour the mixture into your baking tray and smooth the surface with a spatula or the back of a spoon, then bake for about 20 minutes, until the cake is golden and springs back when pressed.

Run a knife around the edge of the tin, turn the cake on to a cooling rack and leave to cool completely. Once completely cool, cut out 8cm diameter circles from your sponge. We use a cookie cutter, but a knife around a tumbler is fine.

To make the brown sugar Italian meringue:
Put the egg whites and 1 tablespoon of the caster sugar into the bowl of a stand mixer, fitted with the whisk attachment, or use a clean glass bowl with a hand-held whisk. Don't start whisking yet.

Put the remaining caster sugar, light brown sugar and water into a heavy-based saucepan and place over a medium/high heat (Don't stir, as this can cause the sugar to crystallize and you'll get crunchy bits in your meringue). Once the sugar has dissolved and the mixture is boiling, attach a sugar thermometer to the pan and continue to boil without stirring until the syrup reaches 120°C. Then take the pan off the heat.

CONTINUES OVERLEAF ›

————————————

Now turn the mixer on to high speed and whisk the egg whites until stiff peaks form. Reduce the speed to low and carefully pour in the hot sugar syrup in a very slow steady stream. Be careful to add the syrup directly to the egg whites, without it touching the side of the bowl or the whisk on the way down, otherwise it will cool before it hits the eggs. Once all the syrup has been added, turn the mixer on to high speed and keep mixing until the sides of the bowl feel cool.

To assemble:
Place your sponge circles in your desired serving dish. Using an ice cream scoop, place a perfect scoop of mojito sorbet on each sponge circle. Working quickly, cover the sorbet and sponge with Italian meringue — a mini palette knife is useful here. Blowtorch to a golden caramel colour and serve immediately with a cocktail umbrella.

BALSAMIC CHERRY PARTY PAVLOVA

SERVES 10

For the labneh (this takes 24 hours to make, but you can use plain Greek yoghurt if you are in a rush):
· 1.2kg thick Greek yoghurt
· ½ tsp sea salt
· 1 tbsp runny honey

· 1 batch of Meringue Girls Mixture (see page 204)

For the macerated cherries:
· 60ml balsamic vinegar
· 110g caster sugar
· 300g fresh cherries, halved, and stones removed

To decorate:
· 400g fresh cherries (keep the stalks on for decoration)
· a splash of kirsch (optional – if you have it hanging around in the booze cabinet)
· 100g slivered pistachios (see suppliers, page 220)

It wouldn't be a Meringue Girls cookbook without a pav in there somewhere, would it? In this recipe, we soak cherries in a sweet balsamic syrup and serve them with salty labneh (a homemade strained yoghurt). The outcome is a deep crunchy meringue shell with a deliciously sweet, sour, salty and umami filling.

Start by making your labneh. Line a large colander with cheesecloth or muslin. Stir the salt into the yoghurt and pour into the cheesecloth/muslin. Set the colander over a bowl, to catch the liquid that drains off. Leave to drain for 24 hours in the fridge, then transfer the resulting thick yoghurt into a bowl, fold in the honey and set aside.

Make your Meringue Girls Mixture.

Preheat the oven to 100°C/gas ½ and line a small baking sheet with baking paper.

Spoon the Meringue Girls Mixture into the centre of the baking sheet and mould into a 25cm spiky circle with your spoon. Using the back of the spoon, make a deep dip in the centre of the mound, forming a large well. Bake in the oven for about 3 hours. When cooked, the meringue should have a firm base and come away from the baking paper. Set aside to cool.

To make the macerated cherries, heat the balsamic vinegar and sugar in a saucepan over a medium heat. Once the sugar has dissolved, turn the heat to low and allow to reduce slightly. Add the prepared cherries and take the pan off the heat. Take the cherries out with a slotted spoon, and reduce the balsamic syrup a little further until it has a nice shiny and drizzly consistency.

If you want an extra kick, soak the cherries for your decoration in the kirsch for 10 minutes before assembling the pavlova.

Place your meringue in the centre of your serving platter. Spoon the honey labneh into the well in the centre and let some ooze down the sides. Scatter with the balsamic cherries, drizzle with balsamic syrup, decorate with the fresh or kirsch-soaked cherries and finish with a sprinkling of slivered pistachios.

PEANUT BUTTER AND JELLY CHOCOLATE FONDANTS

MAKES 4

· cocoa powder, for dusting
· 200g dark chocolate, chopped
· 100g unsalted butter, cut into small pieces
· 2 free-range eggs
· 2 extra egg yolks (keep the egg whites for making meringues)
· 110g caster sugar
· 35g plain flour, sifted
· 1 tsp peanut butter per mould (smooth or crunchy, your choice, or use your own homemade nut butter, see page 33)
· 1 tsp strawberry jam per mould

Equipment:
· 4 dariole moulds

Every time we make this recipe we die and go to heaven. Peanut butter and chocolate is a classic combination, but the ooey-gooey peanut and jelly centre propels these fondants to the next level.

Preheat the oven to 200°C/gas 7. Grease four dariole moulds and dust them with cocoa powder. Do this neatly, as it's the key to a good rise.

Place the chocolate and butter in a saucepan over a gentle heat and stir until the chocolate is melted. Cool to room temperature (otherwise it will scramble the eggs in the next step).

Put the eggs, extra yolks and sugar into a bowl and stir until combined. Stir in the cooled chocolate mixture and the flour.

Spoon the mixture into the moulds until it fills them halfway. Carefully add your peanut butter and jam, right in the centre of each mould. Spoon the remaining mixture around the sides, so that it encases the peanut and jam filling. Fill to just below the top line. Don't overfill, as the fondants will rise during baking. Give the lip of the mould a wipe, to ensure your fondants have the perfect rise.

If you are making these for a dinner party, you can prepare them up to this point an hour before your guests arrive, then pop them into the oven when you are ready to eat dessert.

Place the moulds on a baking tray on the middle shelf of the oven, and bake for 14 minutes, or until the fondants are risen and spring back to the touch. Take them out of the oven and leave to cool for a minute or two, so that the moulds are easier to handle and the mixture continues to cook slightly. To remove, gently loosen the edges with a knife, then place a plate on top and gently flip over. Dust with cocoa powder to serve.

Enjoy immediately. Watch that molten centre ooze.

MERINGUE KISS
ÎLES FLOTTANTES

MAKES 4

For the rhubarb:
· 4 sticks of rhubarb
  cut into 6cm sticks.
· A sprinkle of caster sugar

For the custard:
· 600ml milk
· 1 vanilla pod
· 6 egg yolks
· 100g caster sugar

For the meringue:
· 300ml milk, to poach
· ¼ batch Meringue Girls
  Mixture (see page 204);
  use the rest of the batch to
  make kisses (see page 207)
· pink food colouring
· ½ tsp ground ginger

To top:
· 100g pink and white sugared
  almonds (some roughly
  chopped, some finely
  blitzed)

This is a classic French dessert meaning 'floating islands', given a little Meringue Girls spin. It would be our desert island dessert: pink ginger kisses, roasted rhubarb, custard and sugared almonds – what's not to love?

There are quite a few steps with this, but don't be scared – take your time and keep your cool. You can roast the rhubarb, crush the sugared almonds and make the custard all in advance, so all you have to do is poach your meringues before serving.

To roast the rhubarb:
Preheat the oven to 180°C/gas 6 and butter a deep roasting dish.

Combine the rhubarb and sugar in the buttered roasting dish and roast for 15 minutes, until just cooked. Don't overcook your rhubarb — you want it to keep its shape as much as possible.

To make the custard:
Put the milk into a non-stick saucepan. Split the vanilla pod and scrape the seeds into the milk. Add the empty vanilla pod too, to release the extra flavour. Heat gently, and simmer for 5 minutes. Take off the hob and let the milk cool slightly.

Put the egg yolks and sugar into a bowl and whisk to combine. Slowly, very slowly, pour in the warmed milk, making sure you keep whisking constantly. Return the whole thing to the saucepan and cook over a gentle heat until slightly thickened. This should take about 10 minutes. Be careful not to let it boil, or your custard will curdle. Once done, it should coat the back of your spoon. Strain through a sieve into a clean bowl, to get rid of the vanilla pod. Place a layer of clingfilm directly on the surface of the custard to prevent a skin from forming. The custard can now be stored in the fridge for 2—3 days, until you are ready to use it.

To make your meringue:
Before you make your meringue, prepare your desserts by spooning your custard into the bottom of your serving bowls or glasses, then place a layer of rhubarb on top. The dish is traditionally served at room temperature, but if you like you can heat the custard before serving.

CONTINUES OVERLEAF ›

Pour the poaching milk into a large, wide shallow saucepan over a medium heat, and bring to a simmer.

Make your Meringue Girls Mixture. Now turn a disposable piping bag inside out and paint three stripes on it with pink food colouring. Turn it the right way round again.

Fold the ground ginger into your Meringue Girls Mixture without knocking any air out. Pop your meringue mixture into the striped bag and cut a hole about the size of a 50p piece at the end. Very carefully pipe four 3cm lengths of meringue straight into your simmering milk. Use scissors to snip them to size and make sure the meringues are spaced out in the pan as they expand a lot as they poach. Poach for 30 seconds, then gently turn and cook for a further 30 seconds so they're puffed up and firm. Remove them from the milk with a slotted spoon and place carefully on top of the custard and rhubarb. Sprinkle with the chopped sugared almonds and serve immediately.

CRÈME BRÛLÉE 'CRACK' TART

SERVES 8

For the pastry (you can
use shop-bought sweet
shortcrust pastry instead):
· 375g plain flour, plus
   extra for dusting
· ½ tsp salt
· 1 tbsp caster sugar
· 225g unsalted butter, cut
   into cubes
· 4 tbsp ice-cold water
· 1 free-range egg

For the filling:
· 400ml double cream
· 1 vanilla pod
· 4 egg yolks and 1 whole
   egg (keep the whites for
   making meringues)
· 3 tbsp caster sugar

For the sugar shell:
· 100g demerara sugar

Equipment:
· a rectangular tart tin
   with a ridged edge (approx.
   30cm x 20cm x 4cm – we
   bought ours from Lakeland)
· a blowtorch

One, two, three – crack! Breaking into that hard sugar shell reveals creamy custard speckled with vanilla seeds. This is a thing of beauty.

To make the pastry:
Combine the flour, salt and sugar in a bowl or a food processor. Add the cubed butter and rub in or blend until the mixture resembles breadcrumbs.

Mix together the water and egg in a separate bowl and pour into the flour mixture. Using your hands (or the food processor), bring the ingredients together to form a dough. Tip out on to a floured work surface and knead slightly, then wrap in clingfilm and place in the fridge to rest for 30 minutes.

Preheat the oven to 180°C/gas 6. Grease and flour your rectangular tart tin. Roll out your pastry on a lightly flour-dusted cold surface to the thickness of a £1 coin. Drape your rolled pastry over the top of your tart tin and very carefully use a surplus bit of pastry to gently push it into the grooves of the tin. If you have excess bits hanging over the top, leave these for now.

Line the pastry case with baking paper and fill with baking beans. Blind bake in the oven for 20 minutes, then take out of the oven and remove your lining and beans. Pop the case back into the oven for 5 minutes, until the pastry is golden brown all over. Remove from the oven and, while it's still warm, use a knife to carefully cut around the top of the case to get rid of the excess pastry. Allow to cool completely and then remove from the tin and place on a lined flat baking tray.

To make the filling:
Pour the cream into a heavy-based saucepan. Split the vanilla pod and scrape in the seeds, then throw in the pod. Heat until small bubbles begin to form, then remove from the heat and leave to infuse for 5 minutes. Remove the vanilla pod.

In a bowl, beat together the egg yolks, whole egg and sugar. Keep stirring and pour in the cream, mixing until combined. Strain through a sieve into a jug. Pour the custard into the tart case and bake for 18 minutes, until almost set (it should be quite wobbly in the centre but will firm up on cooling). Leave to cool completely, then chill in the fridge for 30 minutes.

To brûlée:
Scatter a third of the demerara sugar evenly all over the top of your custard tart. Blowtorch this first layer, then sprinkle over a little more demerara and continue to blowtorch carefully in batches so that you build up a nice hard shell. Alternatively pop it under the grill until golden-brown and hard. Crack!

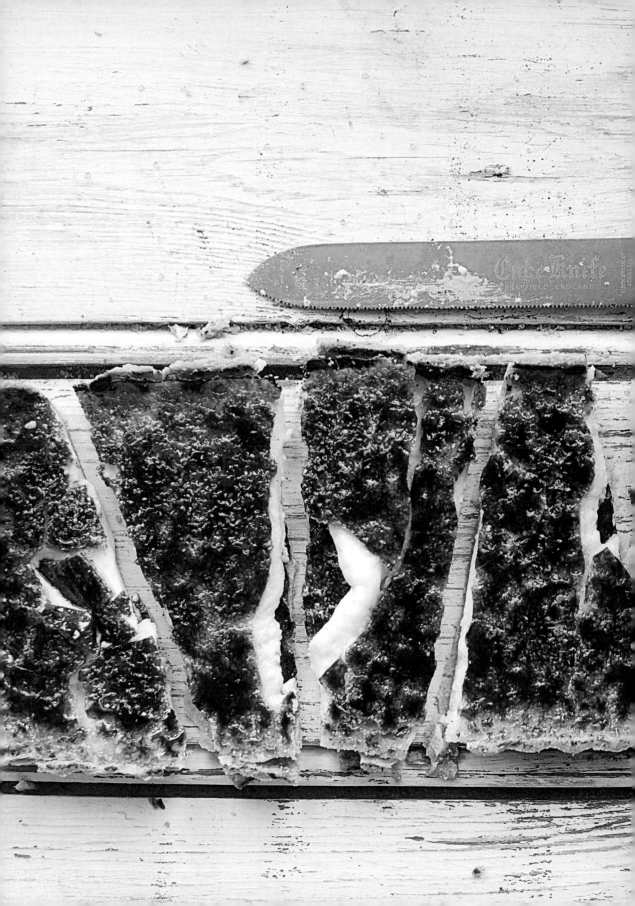

TOTES AMAZEBALLS
CAKE TOPPERS

· 400g high-quality white
  chocolate, chopped
  into very small pieces
  (or you could use candy
  melts, which don't need
  to be tempered, if you
  are in a rush)
· Wilton oil-based food
  colouring (see suppliers,
  page 221) but use it
  sparingly or it can affect
  the taste

Equipment:
· a silicone alphabet mould
  (see suppliers, page 221)
· toothpicks

We discovered this silicone alphabet mould from a gorgeous blog called cococakeland and just couldn't get enough. Check out Lyndsay's blog for the cutest fox face cakes. These chocolate letters are a ridiculously cool way to make big, bold and edible cake toppers. Use to spell out your favourite word – TOTES AMAZEBALLS, I HEART CAKE, OMFG ITS YOUR BDAY.

First you need to temper your white chocolate (see page 216). Working quickly, add a couple of drops of oil-based food colour to the melted chocolate and stir to achieve your ideal colour. Then pour into your chosen letters in the mould. Carefully pop out any air bubbles with a toothpick and scrape off any excess from the top of the mould with a palette knife. Leave to set. (You should leave real tempered chocolate to set at room temperature, as it may lose the wonderful tempered shine you have created if you put it into the fridge.)

If you are using candy melts, simply melt, fill the moulds, and set in the fridge.

You can stir flavours into the chocolate too — just make sure you use oil-based extracts without alcohol, to ensure the chocolate doesn't seize. You can also add freeze-dried fruits, such as raspberries and strawberries.

Use to decorate a show-stopper.

'LET YOUR IMAGINATION RUN WILD' MERINGUE SHARDS

· 1 batch of Meringue
  Girls Mixture (page 204)

Your choice of:
· **Sugarflair or Wilton
  colour pastes (thicker
  colouring is better for
  swirling); but note that
  Wilton colouring can
  affect the taste**
· **dried edible flowers,
  e.g. lavender, blue
  cornflower petals,
  orange calendula petals
  (see suppliers, page 220)**
· **baking sprinkles: hundreds
  and thousands, pearlized
  balls, stars**
· **edible glitter**
· **dried banana chips**
· **nuts: pistachios, hazelnuts,
  flaked almonds**

Equipment:
· **a toothpick**

Meringue shards are the best way to finish off any cake or dessert. Let your imagination run wild by adding bright and fun edible petals and sprinkles to a thin layer of meringue, then bake and snap into huge shards to adorn your creations.

First whip up a quick batch of Meringue Girls mixture. Then turn your oven down to 100°C/gas ½ and line a couple of flat baking trays with non-stick baking paper.

Use a palette knife to spread a 0.5cm layer of meringue mixture all over the baking trays, keeping it as even and as thin as possible. Then let your imagination run wild! Use a toothpick to gently swirl food colours and patterns into the meringue, then sprinkle with your choice of dried edible flowers, baking sprinkles, stars, glitter, dried fruits and nuts.

Bake for 1 hour, or until the whole sheet comes off the baking paper cleanly in one piece. Once ready, remove from the oven and carefully snap into large long shards.

Carefully push these into the top of your cake for the ultimate finishing touch.

EDIBLE ORIGAMI DECORATIONS

· edible rice paper
  (easybake rice paper
  can be bought in lots of
  different colours, see
  suppliers, page 220)
· your choice of origami
  pattern (there are
  thousands of exciting
  patterns online,
  from flamingos to
  pineapples!)

Optional added flourishes:
· edible glitter, with a
  touch of edible glue or
  liquid glucose to make
  sure it sticks to the paper
· edible bronze/gold
  shimmer spray

Simple rice paper fans really give that added wow factor to the top of a cake. For a basic fan, just fold a piece of edible rice paper into a concertina and dip into edible glitter. We've upped the game and created edible origami decorations. This origami fox is super easy and cute – make a whole family, including the little cubs. Or why not make a whole zoo (including flamingos of course!).

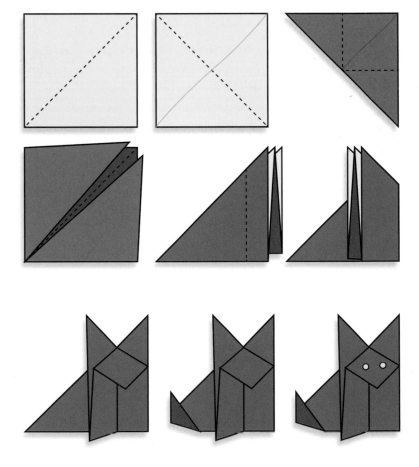

EDIBLE CONFETTI

Equipment:
· a hole-punch
· edible rice paper
  (easybake rice paper
  can be bought in lots of
  different colours, see
  suppliers, page 220)
· edible shimmer spray
  (optional)

Throw this confetti over a cake, at a wedding, or directly into your mouth.

Simply get punching with your hole-punch. You can also use a shaped punch if you like, such as a love heart. If you want to add gold or silver shimmer spray, lightly spray over the rice paper and leave to dry before hole-punching.

For a personalized gift for a foodie friend's wedding, package the confetti up into little bags to hand out to guests. Ideal, as it is bio-degradable.

CRYSTALLIZED FLOWERS

· your choice of edible
flowers (either home-
grown, or buy online
from Greens of Devon,
see suppliers, page 220)
· 1 free-range egg white,
loosened with a drop of
cold water
· caster sugar, for dusting

Equipment:
· a clean paintbrush

We love edible flowers – they are the ideal way to completely beautify your creations. Just like all delicious things, edible flowers are seasonal and have an annoyingly short shelf life. Crystallizing is the ideal way to preserve them so that you can use them all year round. There are so many varieties of edible petals, and it's fab to sow your own. We particularly like borage, cornflowers, chive flowers, pea shoots, violas, rose petals, pansies, primroses, scented geraniums, calendulas and dahlias. For a really unique gift for a lover of baking, package up your crystallized flowers in cute vintage jars.

Carefully paint the entire surface of the petals with the egg whites, making sure to cover both top and bottom. Handling them gently, sprinkle caster sugar from a height to cover both sides of the petals completely.

Leave to dry at room temperature on a piece of baking paper overnight, then use as decoration or store airtight for up to a year.

BACK TO BASICS

MERINGUE GIRLS MIXTURE

**ONE BATCH
MAKES AROUND
40 KISSES,
1 PAVLOVA, OR
6 BIG ONES**

½ batch:
· **150g caster sugar**
· **75g egg whites (from
about 2½ eggs)**

1 batch:
· **300g caster sugar**
· **150g egg whites (from
about 5 eggs)**

Double batch:
· **600g caster sugar**
· **300g egg whites (from
about 10 eggs)**

This is our mother mixture. We use this method whenever we make our meringue kisses, giant meringues, pavlovas and decorative festive meringues. Our mixture is foolproof and so easy to remember – it's a 2:1 ratio of sugar and egg whites.

Preheat your oven to 200°C/gas 7. Line a small baking tray with baking paper, pour in the caster sugar and heat it in the oven for 7 minutes. Heating the sugar helps to create a glossy, stable mixture. Pour the egg whites into the bowl of a stand mixer and whisk them slowly, allowing small stabilizing bubbles to form, then increase the speed until the egg whites form stiff peaks.

Time the sugar and the egg whites so that the sugar is hot, and the egg whites are stiff, AT THE SAME TIME.

Take the sugar out of the oven and turn the oven down to 100°C/gas ½. With your mixer on full speed, very slowly spoon the hot sugar into the stiffly beaten egg whites, making sure the mixture comes back up to stiff peaks after each addition of sugar. Once you have added all the sugar, continue to whisk on full speed until you have a smooth, stiff and glossy mixture. You should continue to whisk for at least 5 minutes once all the sugar has been incorporated. Feel a bit of the mixture between your fingers; if you can still feel the gritty sugar, keep whisking at full speed until it has dissolved and the mixture is smooth, stiff and glossy.

Now you are ready to go!

If you want to make kisses with your Meringue Girls Mixture, spoon your meringue into a disposable piping bag and cut the tip off (to make a hole about the size of a 50p coin). Pipe out your kisses by keeping the bag tight, straight and directly above your baking tray. Squeeze from a 2cm height above the baking tray, then let go with your squeezing hand before pulling up to form the lovely peaks.

Bake for 35–45 minutes, or until the base of the meringues comes off the baking paper clean.

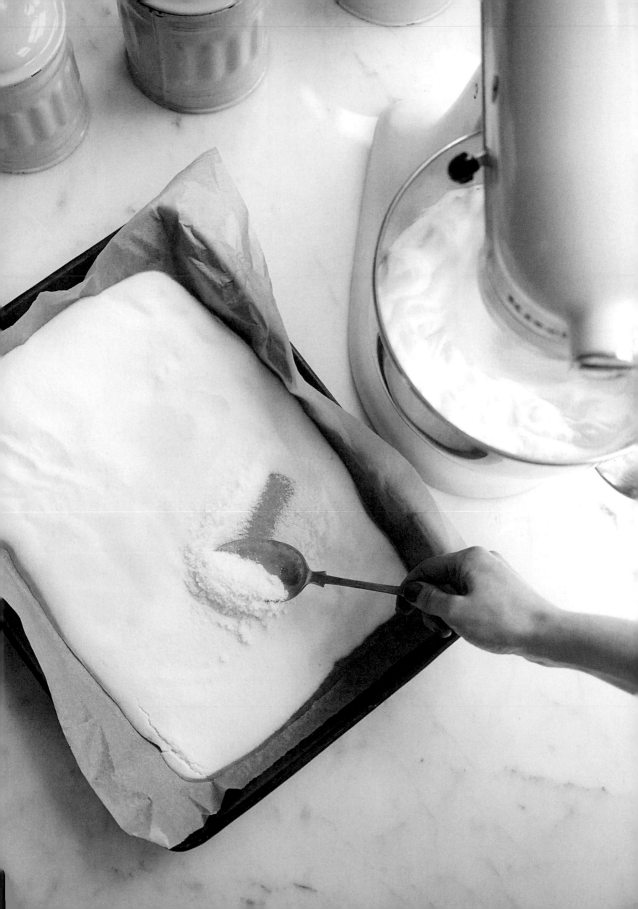

COLOURING, PIPING AND FLAVOURING KISSES

Meringue kisses are the backbone of our bakery business. In our first book they were centre stage and in this book we use them often to decorate our incredible layer cakes, for example those on pages 83 and 103. But you can use them to decorate whatever you choose. Kisses are a fun way to shape and colour meringues.

COLOURING

To colour the kisses, make a batch of uncooked Meringue Girls Mixture (see page 204), and turn a piping bag inside out. Place the bag over a jug or bottle so that it holds itself up. Using food colouring and a clean paintbrush, paint thick stripes from the tip of your piping bag to halfway down the bag (about 5 stripes).

Turn the piping bag right side out and fold back the rim. Carefully spoon your stiff meringue mixture into the piping bag and turn it fully right side out. You need to pack the meringue mixture in tightly, ensuring there are no air bubbles. With sharp scissors, cut off the tip of the piping bag to make a hole the size of a 50p coin.

To get the piping bag flowing, use some of the mixture to pipe small dollops on to the 4 corners of your baking sheets and use these like glue to stick your baking paper to the sheet.

Now you are ready to start piping!

PIPING

Hold the piping bag with both hands, placing your dominant hand at the top of the piping bag and your other hand halfway down the bag. Use the top hand to apply pressure and the lower hand to control the flow of the kisses. Squeeze the bag (like an udder!) to form the kisses. They should have a 5cm diameter and a big peak at the top. This takes practice, so don't worry if you don't get it right the first time.

You can use different nozzles for different effects. For example, a star nozzle will give you beautiful little star-like kisses.

CONTINUES PAGE 210 ›

FLAVOURING

Traditionally, meringues have simply been flavoured with chocolate, vanilla or nuts. But you don't just have to stick with those — we've had a great time experimenting in the kitchen.

Meringue mixture is temperamental, so you need to work quickly. Be careful not to add too much flavouring, such as oily nuts or liquid, as it will deflate the mixture. We've come up with some winning flavours to try below, but feel free to experiment with your own — Willy Wonka style!

For all the flavours that follow we have used one batch of Meringue Girls Mixture.

Chocolate: Use 3 tbsp of good-quality 70% cocoa powder. Fold a third (1 tbsp) into your meringue mixture until just combined. Spoon the mixture into your piping bag, cut the tip and start piping. Once you have piped out all your chocolate kisses, dust the top of the meringues with the remaining cocoa.

Nuts: Nuts have an extremely high oil content that doesn't work well with meringue. You must be extremely sparing with how many ground nuts you fold through the actual mixture.

The are so many different nuts that taste great with meringue — coconut, hazelnut, pistachio, walnut etc. Use 50g of ground nuts, fold 1 tsp of nuts through your Meringue Girls Mixture until just combined, paint the inside of your piping bag with stripes of your choice of natural or unnatural food colouring, then spoon the mixture into your piping bag, cut the tip and start piping. Once you have piped out your nutty kisses smother with the remaining nuts.

Essences: You must be very sparing with how much essence you use as adding any liquid/oil based essences can deflate the meringue mix and contribute to cracking once baked. There is such a wide range of interesting natural essences available, from passionfruit and caramel to watermelon and rose.

Fold in ½ tsp or 3–4 drops of natural essence into your meringue mixture until just combined. Paint stripes in the inside of your piping bag with natural colouring of your choice, spoon the mixture into your piping bag, cut the tip and start piping.

Freeze-dried powders: Freeze-dried powders are an amazing discovery. They are the perfect thing to add to meringues as they are completely dry and usually have quite a sour note which works perfectly with the sweet meringue mixture.

There are so many different types of freeze-dried fruits available, from raspberry and banana to beetroot and passionfruit.

Use 3 tbsp of freeze-dried fruit ground into a fine powder. Fold this into your meringue mixture until just combined. Paint the inside of your piping bag with stripes of your choice of natural food colouring, then spoon the mixture into your piping bag, cut the tip and start piping.

Vanilla: Split 1 whole vanilla pod lengthways and scrape out the seeds. Fold them into your meringue mixture until just combined, making sure the seeds are evenly dispersed. Spoon the mixture into your piping bag, cut the tip and start piping.

The flavour possibilities for meringues are endless — honey, blueberry, cinnamon, ginger, coconut, green tea — just stick to the rules and get your creative juices flowing. Imagine Bounty (chocolate and coconut) or Ferrero Rocher (hazelnut and chocolate). Or try adding a teaspoon of strong natural essence: there are loads to try, like white peach, yuzu, cranberry, apple, lemon or cherry.

ITALIAN MERINGUE

MAKES ENOUGH TO COVER 1 BIG CAKE

· 225g caster sugar
· 6 tbsp tap water
· 4 free-range egg whites
  (approx. 120g if using
  liquid egg whites)

Equipment:
· a sugar thermometer

This is a beautifully glossy, stiff and versatile meringue. This Italian method involves making a sugar syrup, which is then added to the stiff egg whites to cook the meringue on the spot. It's great, as there is no need to bake it, so it has tons of uses – from icing cakes, to smothering baked Alaskas. It can seem really scary to make, but we promise after giving it a go once, you'll never look back.

Put the sugar and water into a small heavy-based saucepan and attach a sugar thermometer to the pan, if you have one. Slowly bring the mixture to the boil over a medium-high heat. Do not stir! Have a pastry brush and a cup of cold water on hand to wash down any sugar crystals that get stuck to the sides of the pan. If you let them build up or if you stir, they will start to crystallize and won't make a smooth sugar syrup.

The sugar is ready when it reaches 120°C on the sugar thermometer. If you don't have a thermometer, test the syrup by dropping a small teaspoonful into a cup of cold water; it should set into a firm ball that can be squashed between your fingers. If it just dissolves into the water, the syrup is not hot enough. If it sets into a hard ball that can't be squished, then it is too hot for making Italian meringue.

Time the syrup and the egg whites, so that the syrup is at the right temperature, and the egg whites are stiff, AT THE SAME TIME. To do this, while the syrup is heating, whisk the egg whites on a low speed in the bowl of a stand mixer until frothy, then when the sugar is nearly hot enough, increase the speed to high and continue whisking until the whites form stiff peaks. As soon as the syrup reaches 120°C, turn the mixer speed to medium and pour the hot syrup in a slow steady stream on to the stiff egg whites. Try not to pour it on to the wire of the whisk or the sides of the bowl — as it will cool quickly, harden and stick to cold metal.

Once you have added all the syrup, return the mixer to high speed until the mixture is stiff and shiny, and the bowl feels cool to the touch — which will take 5–7 minutes. Allow to cool completely before using. Cover with clingfilm until ready to use. Italian meringue can be stored in the fridge for up to 24 hours.

Bellissimo!

'PROPER' CHOCOLATE TEMPERING

DARK

· melting temp: 45-50 ˚C
· cooling temp: 28-29 ˚C
· reheating temp: 31-32 ˚C

MILK

· melting temp: 40-45 ˚C
· cooling temp: 27-28 ˚C
· reheating temp: 30-31 ˚C

WHITE

· melting temp: 40 ˚C
· cooling temp: 24-25 ˚C
· reheating temp: 27-28 ˚C

Equipment:
· digital thermometer

Tempering is the process that stabilizes the cocoa butter in the chocolate and gives it that lovely shine and crisp crack. If you melt chocolate and let it set without tempering, it often turns a streaky matt grey, which isn't very pretty.

We used to be scared of tempering chocolate, as it seemed like a fiddly and difficult thing to do. However, it really isn't. You just need a pan of simmering water with a heatproof glass bowl, a digital thermometer and the three temperature ranges shown left to work with. The outcome will be amazingly professional shiny chocolate.

Tempering chocolate is great if you are making gifts, as it raises the chocolate's melting point, so it keeps a lot longer in perfect shiny condition.

Pour a few centimetres of water into a saucepan and bring it to a simmer over a medium-low heat. Place a heatproof bowl over the pan, making sure its base doesn't come into contact with the water.

Grate your chocolate in a food processor or by hand with a grater, or chop it very finely with a knife.

Place roughly two-thirds (just do this by eye) of your finely chopped or grated chocolate in the bowl. Stirring regularly, melt the chocolate until you reach 'melting temp' — be careful not to go too much higher than this.

Now remove the bowl from the heat and add the remaining (un-melted) third of your chocolate in small batches. Keep stirring and reading the temperature, adding pieces of chocolate slowly while stirring to get it to the correct 'cooling temp' - you may not need all the rest of the chocolate to get it to the right temperature. Make sure you do not let it go too cold.

When it's at its 'cooling temp', place the bowl back on the pan and, while stirring, reheat it to its 'reheating temp'. Your chocolate is now good to go!

You need to use melted and tempered chocolate quickly, as it only stays in temper for as long as it remains within this final 'reheated' temperature range.

Remember to let the chocolate set in a cool place at room temperature — not in the fridge, as this can often make your chocolate bloom with a white sheen, and lose the lovely shine you have created.

EASY-PEASY TEMPERING

· couverture chocolate drops
  or good quality shop-bought
  chocolate bars

This type of tempering is a little less accurate, but it's good if you don't have a digital thermometer or much time. If you are very careful to heat the chocolate gently, there is no need to re-temper (i.e. use a digital thermometer to heat the chocolate to the three exact temperature ranges), as the original temper will not be lost. It is all about keeping the original formation of the fat molecules in place and not scrambling them with too much heat! The original chocolate maker did the hard work, you just need to keep that temperature low.

You can do this in a bain-marie – a heatproof glass bowl placed over a pan of gently simmering water. Or in a microwave on a very low setting in a microwaveable plastic bowl.

All good shop-bought bars will be tempered already – you can easily tell, as they will have a nice 'snap' when they're broken and will be shiny. We use tempered couverture chocolate drops in the bakery, as they can be heated quickly and consistently.

Use couverture drops, or grate your good-quality white, dark or milk chocolate into fine pieces. Grating the bar, or using little button drops, means that it melts faster, so is less likely to overheat and lose its original temper. If you are grating a lot of chocolate, it's quicker to just blitz it in a food processor until it's in little bits.

Place roughly two-thirds (just do this by eye) of the grated chocolate in a microwaveable plastic bowl (not glass, as glass conducts too much heat in the microwave and will continue to cook the chocolate when you don't want it to).

Put your microwave on its lowest setting, and heat the chocolate in 10-second blasts. Take the bowl out and stir after each blast. It will take around five 10-second sessions to melt the chocolate. You want it so that it JUST melts when you stir it. If you are doing it on the hob, place the chocolate in a heatproof glass bowl over a bain-marie and stir until it JUST melts.

Now add the reserved one-third of melted chocolate and stir until it melts. You may need to give it another 5-second burst in the microwave, or one more stir over a bain-marie, until it all comes together. You are now ready to use it!

Remember to let the chocolate harden and cool at room temperature, not in the fridge.

SUPPLIERS

INGREDIENTS

> Agave syrup: Ocado.com
> Baking sprinkles, e.g. hundreds & thousands, pearlized balls: Waitrose have a good selection of bakery bling
> Chocolate drops: Callebaut pre-tempered drops, from ChocolateTradingCo.com
> Candy melts: Yolli.com
> Cocoa nibs: Ocado.com
> Coconut flour: Tiana, from Ocado.com
> Coyo yoghurt: Ocado.com
> Crystallized flowers and sugared petals: uncleroys.co.uk, who do a huge selection of dried petals, e.g. rose, carnation, marigold, hibiscus, cornflower, lavender and violet
> Edible gold glitter: Rainbow Dust or Stardust, from Ocado.com
> Edible metallic gold food paint: Rainbow Dust, from Amazon.co.uk
> Edible rice paper: Easybake, from CakeCraftShop.co.uk
> Edible silver and gold leaf: Souschef.co.uk
> Edible flowers: fresh, from GreensOfDevon.com; dried, from theedibleflowershop.co.uk
> Freeze-dried powders: exciting flavours, e.g. passionfruit and banana, from Souschef.co.uk
> Freeze-dried raspberries and strawberries: Ocado.com
> Fruity confetti baking sprinkles: Ocado.com
> Gluten-free baking powder and bicarbonate of soda: Doves Farm, from Ocado.com
> Honey: fresh honeycomb in honey from Middle Eastern supermarkets; Rowse cutcomb honey from Ocado.com
> Liquid glucose: Ocado.com
> Liquid egg white: Two Chicks, from Ocado.com
> Liquorice: Mr Stanley's Liquorice Pipes, from Ocado.com
> Mojito sorbet: Lushice, from Ocado.com
> Natural essences: great range from foodieflavours.com; lakeland.co.uk also has a good natural range
> Nut butters: Meridian, from Ocado.com
> Pashmak Persian Fairy Floss: HarveyNichols.com, Selfridges.com
> Pearl sugar: Ocado.com, Souschef.co.uk
> Pistachio slivers: Souschef.co.uk
> Popping candy: coated, from Souschef.co.uk; Heston uncoated popping candy, from Ocado.com; Fizz Wiz, from cybercandy.co.uk

> Soft liquorice: Panda, from Ocado.com
> Vanilla pods: Souschef.co.uk, Amazon.co.uk
> Wilton oil based food colourings: Amazon.co.uk

Note: We only use 100% natural colourings derived from fruit and vegetables in our meringues. For the bakery we use a wholesale supplier and buy in bulk. For a home baking scale we recommend Lakeland's natural colour range (Lakeland.co.uk). In the book, we've used natural where possible, but sometimes to get magical bright effects you need to delve into the unnatural world, e.g. Wilton or Sugarflair, but be aware that Wilton colours can affect taste so use sparingly.

EQUIPMENT

> Blowtorch: Nisbets.co.uk
> Cake tins, including square: Lakeland.co.uk
> Cellophane sweetie bags with silver card bases: bagnboxman.co.uk, Amazon.co.uk
> Chocolate thermometer, sugar thermometer: Lakeland.co.uk
> Cookie cutters: Lakeland.co.uk
> Ramekins: Lakeland.co.uk
> Ice lolly rocket moulds: Kitchencraft.co.uk
> Jam jars: Lakeland.co.uk
> Lollipop sticks: Yolli.com
> Marbling paints: craft stores, Amazon.co.uk
> Muslin cloth: Mothercare.com, Amazon.co.uk
> Piping bags: 21 inch Savoy disposable blue piping bags, from Amazon.co.uk
> Piping nozzles: Lakeland.co.uk
> Plastic pipettes: Amazon.co.uk
> Pyramid chocolate moulds: shopchefrubber.com, Souschef.co.uk
> 3-bar silicone chocolate mould — Amazon.co.uk
> Pyramid silicone mould: Nisbets.co.uk
> Rectangular tart case: Lakeland.co.uk
> Silicone alphabet chocolate moulds: Yolli.com

MINI MASTERCLASSES

TINS

To save you needing to buy loads of different sized cake tins, we've created all the layered cakes in this book using two round tins of the same size: 18cm diameter. This size of tin has a depth of 5cm, which allows you to split each cake in half across the middle, ending up with four layers. This gives a lovely height to your cakes and makes them look really impressive when cutting. You can of course scale any of the recipes up or down to make them bigger or smaller, depending on how many people you want to feed. Just remember that you want to fill your tin to no more than halfway up, to allow enough room for the cake to rise.

HOW TO FILL AND COAT CAKES

With the cakes in this book, we split each of them in half using a cake leveller (available from cake-decorating suppliers such as Lakeland). However, if you don't have one of these, a long bread knife will work well too — cut the cake in half as straight as possible (you can use cocktail sticks pushed in at intervals to keep you on track!). We then filled each layer using a cranked palette knife (this is one which has a bend in it to prevent your hand from getting messy), using long, firm, spreading motions to get an even layer of filling.

Once the layers are filled and stacked, start coating the sides of the cake with the same palette knife, starting from the base of the cake and working your way to the top — if your buttercream starts to pull on the crumbs, soften it for a few seconds in the microwave and it should glide on a lot easier. Apply more or less pressure to the palette knife to create thicker or thinner layers of buttercream.

Once all the sides are coated, cover the top of the cake last, then refrigerate for around 20 minutes to allow the buttercream to firm up.

CONTINUES OVERLEAF ›

FAVE EQUIPMENT

We've put together an equipment list of super-useful cake-making bits which will all help to make your cakes look really professional. You don't necessarily need to buy all of these, but we wanted to let you know what we use so that you can get started. The tools are generally stocked by most cake-decorating suppliers, as well as high street shops.

> Cake leveller — Glide one of these babies through your cake using a saw action and you'll never have wonky cakes again!
> Cranked palette knife — Makes filling and covering your cakes a total breeze.
> Mini palette knife — Excellent for trimming, cutting and spreading stuff.
> Smoother — Really handy if you decide to tackle the Fondant Fox cake (see page 91), as this will make your fondant finish so-o-o perfect.
> Sugar thermometer (a digital one is easiest) — really handy for making sugar syrups to use in things like Italian meringue.
> Turntable — Allows you to stay in the same position when decorating your cakes — just give it a whirl.
> Chocolate tempering spatula — Really useful for keeping an eye on chocolate temperatures while heating/cooling. It's a spatula and thermometer combined.

TROUBLE-SHOOTING TIPS

Here are some tips we wanted to give you on a few common baking mistakes that can easily happen, to help you get perfect results each time.

CAKES

Not risen: If your cake hasn't risen enough, this is generally because the butter and sugar haven't been creamed for long enough. Creaming creates lots of tiny air pockets, which fill with steam when baking — therefore if it hasn't been creamed for long enough, there won't be as many air pockets. This should take anything from 5 to 10 minutes (depending on whether you're using a hand-held or a stand mixer), and the butter should have turned really pale in colour — almost white.

Split/curdled: If your cake mix splits, this is generally because one of the ingredients is too cold. Before you start baking, ensure all your ingredients are at room temperature. It could also be that you are adding your eggs too quickly, so slow down and add them in a steady stream. If splitting does happen at any time along the way, add a tablespoon of flour to the mixture and that should bring it back together.

Cracked: This usually happens because the oven is too hot, so you may need to lower the temperature. However, sometimes cracking on top of the cake is totally normal, particularly if the mixture contains liquid (for example buttermilk), as the cracks are where the moisture is released during baking.

Sunk middle: This is when the cake rises in the oven too quickly and can't support the weight so sinks in the middle — double-check that you haven't added too much raising agent (such as bicarbonate of soda or baking powder), as that's normally the reason this happens.

BUTTERCREAM

When covering a cake with buttercream, sometimes cake crumbs find their way in — to prevent this, try baking your cake the day before you want to ice it (so that the cake sponge isn't too soft). It may also be because your buttercream is too stiff — try adding a touch more milk and re-beat, or pop it into the microwave for a few seconds to soften.

CONTINUES OVERLEAF ›

MERINGUES

There isn't a meringue mishap we haven't experienced — whether they crack, flop, turn wrinkly and sticky or simply refuse to bake . . . we've seen it all! Here are our tips for avoiding the main pitfalls:

> When flavouring your Meringue Girls Mixture, be sparing with essences, nuts and anything oily. A little goes a long way, and a light hand here makes a big difference! With nuts, cocoa, etc., add minimal amounts to the mixture and sprinkle loads on top.
> Once your mixture is ready to pipe, get piping! The longer the mixture sits around, the more it deflates and loses all that lovely air you patiently whisked in. Paint your piping bag and get your baking tray ready in advance.
> Make sure your oven, baking trays and silicone mats are completely dry — water leads to steam, which can cause the kisses to come out wrinkly.
> Avoid slamming or opening and closing the oven door too often — an even temperature helps avoid cracked meringues.
> Check the oven temperature using a separate thermometer.

LOLLIPOPS

Dark: If your lollies turn dark in colour, this generally means the syrup has either been overheated (i.e. temperature too high) or heated for too long. Always keep a close eye on your sugar syrup while heating.

Cloudy: If the lollies are cloudy, you may have stirred your sugar syrup, adding impurities to the sugar crystals.

MARSHMALLOWS

If your marshmallows don't set, double-check that the quantity of gelatine you added is correct, as brands vary. It may also be because the egg whites weren't stiff enough before adding the sugar syrup — or that the sugar syrup wasn't hot enough, so be extra sure on all of these!

If the marshmallows crack when you twist them, this may be because you piped them too thinly (so cut the end of your piping bag higher up) or because they started to set too much before they were twisted.

CHOCOLATE

Working with chocolate can be tricky, so here are a few tips to help you:

Blooming: This is when the chocolate hardens dull, with small white dots all over it. This is normally due to the chocolate temperature being changed rapidly, so let your chocolate harden at room temperature (not in the fridge). Also it could be because the chocolate has been left to go hard, then has been reheated too drastically. If chocolate completely sets, you need to start the tempering process again. Also, make sure you're using a mould that is super-clean and grease-free — give it a polish with kitchen towel for really shiny results.

Seizing/splitting: This happens when the cocoa butter in chocolate overheats. If using a microwave to temper your chocolate, stir between blasts — and if heating in a bowl over a saucepan, stir constantly and keep an eye on temperature. Also you can only add oil-based essences and colours to chocolate. Water-based ones will make the chocolate seize.

CHOUX PASTRY

If your choux pastry cracks, this will be because you over-mixed your butter/flour/water (this is called a panade). Just ensure you stop mixing as soon as it's smooth. If the choux pastry does not rise, this will be because not enough egg has been added, so make sure you only start adding it once the panade is at room temperature — if it's too hot or too cold it won't absorb enough egg.

GOLD AND SILVER LEAF

This is impressive stuff when added to cakes and sweets — however, it can be frustrating to transfer from the packet! Never touch the leaf with your hands, as it will cling to anything with moisture — try lifting it with a clean dry paintbrush or a mini palette knife. If it won't cling to what you want it to, add a tiny bit of glucose syrup to the cake or chocolate and it should stick easily.

THANK YOU

David Loftus (davidloftus.com), for working your magic lens once again.
Rowan Yapp and Square Peg, for continuing to believe in us.
Jesse Holborn (designholborn.co.uk), for the wonderful design of this book.
Jo Harris, for her incredible props styling.

Stacey's husband, Brady, for literally being the best person in the whole wide world. Thank you for being so patient and understanding. I couldn't have got through this last year without you and I just LOVE you, so much. Never forget it. Stacey's parents, Brendan and Sue, for giving me the gift of life, love and happiness. Stacey's sister Sian (sian-o.co.uk), for being the best sister ever and helping us out with all her guru design skills.

Alex's fiancé, Neil, for being the best Dad to our beautiful daughter Indiana, and all round tash man dreamboat. Alex's Mumma and Papa, Nicky and Laurie — love you both more than the Universe. Neil's Mum, Libby Fry, for her wise words and literally getting us through the first six months of the Indi whirlwind! Alan and Jay, for fabulous babysitting and feeding us up. Tim, for sound business advice and much needed R&R. Stacey aka 'Percy', for being the best business partner, you are my WIFEY 4 LIFEY. Thanks for being incredibly supportive throughout my pregnancy and with Indi. Love you forevz. And finally to Indi, I hope you read this in a few years time. I couldn't have wished for a lovelier baby girl.

Sylvia Pearson, our EVERYTHING. A woman of so many talents, patience being her finest. She has been with us from the very beginning through thick and thin and we honestly could not have gotten to where we are today without her. She is undoubtedly the third Meringue Girl. Beki Spencer, the backbone of the business, the keeper of the list and food stylist extraordinaire. Chloe Ride who started as an intern and flourished into so much more, helping us to write, test and style many of these recipes (thecitygirlskitchen.wordpress.com). Carla, aka Fondant Fox (fondantfox.com), the foxiest, most skilful cake baker we know and the master of keeping her cool when things were all a bit much — the FF/MG collaboration was meant to be. Miranda Keeble, our meringue maestro with an amazing eye for design and detail. Rosie Kellett, multi-talented actor, baby-whisperer, star piper — we're so glad you walked into the bakery that day! Danielle Coates, total fox with serious chocolate skills. Sam Edyn, our gorgeously kind and cool Meringue Boy. Sarah Hunter, baking pro and all-round sweetheart. Lise Biancotto, our French bombshell and a total star. Bella Tubbs, bubbly babe with big ideas. Rochelle (ohsosweetbaker.com), who was oh so sweet with recipe testing. All work experience past and present, we owe you one. The lovely ladies who we've shared our bakery with: Lotta from Eat Chic (eatchic.co.uk), Adelle from BKD-London (bkd-london.com) and Chloe from Fatties (fattiesbakery.com). To Jerry Cooper and all the Broadway Market Mews Partners for welcoming us with open arms. Gizzi Erskine, for all her ongoing support and generally being AWESOME. Jamie Oliver, for the magical quote for cookbook one and for constantly inspiring us. Ashlee Ackland (sweetheartsandscallywags.co.uk), for the banging MG playlists and pom pom skills. Kim Kiefer, for the magical make up. Green & Blacks (greenandblacks.co.uk) for their fantastic ice cream and chocolate — yum yum! Dean Brettschneider, for all the business advice! Mark Wilderspin for the strategic know-how. Melissa at Squash Banana Design (squashbanana.co.uk) — congrats on the bubba and thanks for your website wizardry. Nisbets (nisbets.co.uk), for their help kitting out our once empty bakery. Lakeland (lakeland.co.uk), for our gorgeous baking kit. Rangemaster (rangemaster.co.uk) for giving us our amazing FX Pro oven. KitchenAid (kitchenaid.co.uk), for our rainbow of mixers which we would be lost without. Partumis Metal (partumis-metal.co.uk) for our gorgeous pink MG gates. To all those who helped us with the BEST cookbook launch party in the world: Kate Woods, Fabulous Feasts and the team at Woods' Silver Fleet (silverfleet.co.uk) — such a stunning venue to float down the Thames on, cocktail in hand. Thank you for your INCREDIBLE generosity. Athena and Mairead of Rebel Rebel Flowers (rebelrebel.co.uk) for the amazing rainbow waterfall of flowers. Gorgeous Gus from augustusbloom.com. Pinkster Gin (pinkstergin.com) and Peter Spanton Tonics (peterspantonbeverages.com) for the VERY fitting PINK gin and the delicious cardamom tonic for our G&Ts. Meantime Beer (meantimebrewing.com) for hooking us up and getting us boozy. To all of our retailers: Selfridges, Harvey Nichols, Fortnum & Mason, Jamie Oliver's Recipease and Broadway Market — thank you for your ongoing support and dedication to our little brand.

INDEX

10 9 8 7 6 5 4 3 2 1

Square Peg, an imprint of Vintage,
20 Vauxhall Bridge Road,
London SW1V 2SA

Square Peg is part of the Penguin Random House group of companies
whose addresses can be found at global.penguinrandomhouse.com

www.vintage-books.co.uk

A CIP catalogue record for this book is available from the British Library

ISBN 9780224101059

Photography by David Loftus
Design by Jesse Holborn, Design Holborn
Illustrations by Niki Pilkington
Prop styling by Jo Harris
Food styling by Stacey O'Gorman and Alex Hoffler

Printed and bound in Germany by Appl Druck

Penguin Random House is committed to a sustainable future for our business, our readers and
our planet. This book is made from Forest Stewardship Council® certified paper